M000031685

Praise for **Player-Coach**

"*Player-Coach* addresses a critical need for both business and HR professionals, offering guidance for individuals transitioning from a role as a subject matter expert to one of a team leader. The four-part leadership model will help functional experts become effective leaders. The authors give readers a blend of real-life stories, essential tips, and insights that take new player-coaches on a journey of developing the critical skills necessary to become excellent leaders, motivators, and mentors."

DEBBIE STOREY, PRESIDENT & CEO, AT&T PERFORMING ARTS CENTER

"Much is written about the challenges faced by those promoted over their peers. By focusing on those who play and coach, Val Markos and Tammy Martin shine a light on the advantages that these leaders have over those rotated into leadership roles. Leaders elevated into the player-coach role are uniquely suited to identify meaningful development opportunities and on-the-job growth experiences to prepare the team for leadership responsibilities. Just another of the tried-and-true insights captured in *Player-Coach!*"

HELENE LOLLIS, PRESIDENT & CEO, PATHBUILDERS

"Val Markos and Tammy Martin provide great insights and practical advice on how to master the tenuous balance between these two critical roles —player and coach. It's definitely worth a read!"

MARC EFFRON, PRESIDENT, THE TALENT STRATEGY GROUP

What do executives say about player-coaches?

"Player-coach is about the work you are doing. Are you one of the team or are you doing others' work? Managing your team is a big part of a coach's job lower in an organization, and then as you progress, the mix of what you do changes."

A TECHNOLOGY EXECUTIVE

"Relinquishing expertise can be an issue for player-coaches and for the organization. Some players will never succeed at being an effective coach because they just *cannot give up being the expert*. And many people get stuck growing as a coach because the *organization* values their expertise and doesn't want to let go of it."

A HUMAN RESOURCES EXECUTIVE

"I was brought into the business because of my experience in litigation; my natural default was to be a player. I was asked to switch gears to non-billable work and that was hard to do. My challenge was to be intentional about 'coach' work. It's like a new muscle that isn't as strong as all the others."

A LEGAL EXECUTIVE

"I've often seen the best salesperson, the best clinician, or the best financial mind getting promoted to coach. Unfortunately, that doesn't always mean the best leader gets promoted."

A HEALTHCARE EXECUTIVE

"Leaders who have been a part of large organizations seem to have an easier time moving from subject matter expert to leader because they've had access to more support mechanisms, like development experiences and training."

A HUMAN RESOURCES EXECUTIVE

"It's a real challenge when some player-coaches want perfection. As a player they may have been able to manage perfection, or what they thought was perfection, as an individual contributor. Managing perfection is difficult when one's scope increases like that of a coach/leader. You have to continually ask yourself on each task: 'Do I have to do that?'"

A FINANCIAL EXECUTIVE

Player-
Coach

Player-

VAL MARKOS PhD
& TAMMY MARTIN

Coach

MOVING FROM SUBJECT MATTER EXPERT TO LEADER AND GETTING THE BEST FROM THE TEAM

PLAYER-COACH
LEADERSHIP PRESS

ISBN 978-1-7333431-0-7 (paperback)
ISBN 978-1-7333431-1-4 (ebook)

Published by Player-Coach Leadership Press
www.playercoachleadership.com

Produced by Page Two
www.pagetwo.com

Cover and interior design by Taysia Louie
Interior illustrations by Jennifer Lum

www.playercoachleadership.com

Some names and identifying details have been changed to protect the privacy of individuals.

CONTENTS

ACKNOWLEDGMENTS

THANK YOU to the many contributors and leaders who helped shape our careers, thoughts, and capabilities. Today's business environment demands more and more from coaches, leaders, and executives, yet the time and resources to support growth for these roles can fall short. From our experiences and interviews with several executives across an array of fields, we were inspired to put into writing a model that highlights the areas of focus one must concentrate on when stepping up from a subject matter expert (player) to a leader (coach) of those in the same or similar expertise. Whether you are the player, a coach, or a supporter, we hope you find this model helpful in your pursuit to lead, encourage, and influence growth and development in future leaders.

To Don Hallacy, Helene Lollis, Patrick Moore, Joey Schultz, Nimesh Shah, Lynette Smith, Monica Smith, and Anna Stevens—your insights and input were invaluable. Thank you for your time and commitment to leading others.

To our families and colleagues, your support is immeasurable.

With all gratitude,

VAL AND TAMMY

INTRODUCTION

I N LATE 2017, I was invited to do a presentation on leadership concepts at a leadership development program. The participants came from a wide variety of companies and industries and had been promoted within their respective staff functions—finance, compliance, legal, human resources (HR), and information technology—and were now function leaders. Helene, the program director, told me that through interviews and background research she had already identified 'work-life balance' and 'people management' as the two most common issues for the group. As an experienced executive coach and corporate human resources professional, I knew exactly what she was talking about.

Based on my own research, I know that it is a common occurrence for new subject matter experts to struggle in their role because they believe that their *value* is their expertise, and that belief can get in the way of their *leadership* role. They don't realize that their new role is more about *coaching* others to do the work than the *application of their expertise*. After all, I experienced the same thing when I started my career after eight years of college and graduate school: I stepped into a *leadership* position after years of training to be an *expert*. I knew all about the pressures—often self-imposed—of needing to be a leader while still being looked upon to provide subject matter expertise.

This concept became the inspiration for my presentation, that portion of the session was titled 'Player-Coach,' and I wove some aspects of what has become our player-coach model into the discussion. The concept and the model were both very well received. As I was presenting, a young participant raised her hand and mentioned how relevant and helpful this discussion was to her. She also asked, "Where can I continue to learn about this concept of being an effective player-coach?" I told her I didn't know of anything off the top of my head, but I would be glad to find her some resources.

After the session, Helene approached me, congratulated me on my successful presentation, and proclaimed, "Good luck finding some resources! I do a lot of reading and your comments on this concept are unique—I haven't heard anyone else touch on this topic." As I left the event, I thought to myself, "I could suggest several *general* leadership books, but nothing that specifically addresses the challenges of a player-coach..." And the idea for this book was born.

I decided to invite my colleague Tammy Martin to join me in this endeavor. We worked together for over a decade at a large Fortune 500 corporation and have witnessed the trajectory of many player-coaches—some extremely successful, and some very disappointing—and Tammy has coached and managed many more in her continued career. We have witnessed the struggles and celebrated and praised those who excelled at developing into great player-coaches.

VAL

MY LEADERSHIP JOURNEY is different from Val's. My degree is in journalism with an emphasis in graphic arts. During college, and for three years post-college, I was truly developing my skills in journalism/graphic arts. In the early 1980s, before Macs and PowerPoint, I was offered a graphic arts position in the large corporation Val mentioned. Graphic arts was not a core competency of the company, but rather a specialty that saved the company money. In fact, in the beginning, only two people in a company of 100,000 employees performed the role. As the demand for our group's skills grew within the company, our team expanded to almost ten. For about a year, I was a player-coach as a graphic artist before I was asked to be the leader of the group. I guess you could say I was a jump-start player-coach!

When the leadership in my department realized I excelled as a manager of people and workflow, I was asked to focus more on leadership than my professional expertise (graphic arts). As our team took on more and more administrative services (copy, mail, supply, graphics, etc.) for the company's headquarters location, I shifted from being a leader of administrative services to leading small- to medium-sized teams in IT, operations, and communications. After about ten years with the company, I joined the human resources (HR) function and never looked back.

As an HR executive responsible for high-potential development and supporting one-third of an organization of over 300,000 employees, I observed and coached numerous player-coaches for twenty years. I was thrilled when Val asked me to join him on this adventure and couldn't wait to share my experiences on the player-coach journey.

TAMMY

WHEN WE STARTED our research for this book, we contacted a number of successful player-coaches who we met through the years and asked them to share some of their most memorable professional experiences and approaches to both playing *and* coaching. Their breadth of knowledge provided us with some new insights, but mostly reinforced the perspectives we provide in the player-coach model, and the skills and behaviors we believe are required of all successful player-coaches.

Exemplary leaders and world changers may be born with it, but most of us have the potential to be more capable leaders, and we can all benefit from improving our leadership skills and actions. We wrote this book to help those subject matter experts who are stepping into leadership roles—or have already assumed them—to be great leaders. We address the player-coach transition and how to progress to the coach role effectively. We also look at the challenges facing the player-coach and describe actions that will help resolve them.

With a little guidance and a few simple concepts, we believe many more experts who are asked to lead other experts can do so more effectively. By 'simple concepts,' we mean that the concepts themselves are not complex or difficult to understand. It is the practice and the discipline of applying them that can be challenging and requires real commitment.

We want to see player-coaches thrive, to think about the leadership aspect of their role. We hope they consider how to apply the principles, skills, and actions we describe in this book so their teams are effective and engaged, and so the individuals who work for them have a positive experience. We hope this book will be of value to those facing the challenges of playing and coaching in the same role, and also to the leaders, supporters, mentors, and sponsors of people making their way through the transition.

For ease of use, the book is organized into three parts. Part One explains the concept of player-coach. Part Two introduces and elaborates on our model for successful player-coaches. Part Three focuses on the critical skills and support systems that are required for player-coaches to be highly effective and continue to grow in their discipline and in leadership strengths.

If you are already a player-coach, or you are moving in that direction, this book is full of information that will add value to for your career trajectory, both directly and indirectly. Even if every concept we introduce isn't specific to your current role, we challenge you to reflect on your work and ask yourself how you might grow and be more effective by considering and implementing the ideas we present.

PART

THE

PLAYER-COACH

ONE

Many athletes become good, even great coaches when they retire from playing. The player-coach does both at the same time: they are on the roster, they get in the game, and they also step out of the player role to coach. It's the same in business: subject matter experts have their own work to do, but they are also put into people management or leadership positions.

1

MOVING FROM
DOING TO *LEADING*

"IT WASN'T UNTIL much later in my life that I learned to appreciate the amazing ability of Bill Russell to not only play the game of basketball, but to coach the Celtics as he was playing. At the time, I wasn't really a Celtics fan. I remember rooting for the 76ers with Wilt Chamberlain and Hal Greer (big man and little guy), or the Lakers with Chamberlain, Elgin Baylor, and Jerry West, but you could not ignore the incredible Celtics with Russell and John Havlicek. While I must have watched Russell and the Celtics battle Chamberlain a half dozen times in a playoff setting, rarely did Chamberlain get the better of the Celtics. Russell always stood out as a team player, and he may not have outscored Chamberlain, but he always led the Celtics to victory."

EXECUTIVE COACH AND AUTHOR

BILL RUSSELL was an incredible basketball player who played center for the Boston Celtics from 1956 to 1969, when they had one of the great dynasties—not only in the National Basketball Association (NBA), but in all of sports. Many still remember watching the Celtics battle it out with the Philadelphia 76ers for NBA supremacy. A five-time MVP and a twelve-time All-Star, Russell won eleven NBA championships during his thirteen-year career. The Celtics of the late 1950s to 1960s—a period referred to as 'the Bill Russell era'—are widely considered to be one of the most dominant teams of all time.[1]

Russell was particularly known for his team play, which was likely influenced by being snubbed in college: he was identified as only the *second-best* center in Northern California, even though he had led his University of San Francisco to the national college title. Russell supposedly told himself he would not allow others to be the judge of his career, so he made a conscious decision to put the team first and let the scores and records stand for themselves.

Russell's accomplishments in his college years or even in his early NBA years aren't well known, but during his thirteen-year run as center for the Celtics, he won eleven NBA titles, and everyone knew him and what he was capable of doing. The

Celtics simply seemed invincible regardless of what the competition threw at them.

Russell was known for his tough defense and being a master of the rebound: it has been said that the Celtics played a 'Hey, Bill!' defense. When anyone struggled to contain the player they were assigned to, they yelled "Hey, Bill!" and Russell was fast enough to help them out, and could even get back to cover his own player if the ball went that way. He was also known to meticulously study the competition's centers, right down to the movement of their feet, in order to successfully defend them.

When renowned Celtics coach Red Auerbach retired after the 1965–1966 season, he asked Bill to replace him. As player-coach, Russell led the Celtics to three playoffs and two NBA championships.

Many athletes become good, even great coaches when their playing days come to an end. The player-coach, like Russell in his final years with the Celtics, does both at the same time. They are on the roster, they get in the game, and they also step out of the player role to coach.

Many of us play or have played that player-coach role in our professional lives: we are subject matter experts with our own work to do, but we are also responsible for people management or leadership positions. There are unlimited examples: general counsels, CFOs, CIOs, CMOs, claims managers, policy/law enforcement personnel, real estate agents, a myriad of specialists in the healthcare industry, and the list goes on. Player-coaches can be found anywhere a subject matter expert moves into a leadership role. They are still sought for their expertise, but they also manage others. They are players *and* coaches at the same time.

This book addresses the concept of playing *and* coaching, and while we'd love to write about sports more than we already have, this book won't go there. Instead, we will apply this concept to leadership in business and other organizations. The player-coach concept is about doing *and* leading, and striking a balance between the two.

The player-coach

A person who performs work and leads others within the same role in an organization is what we refer to as a 'player-coach.' To a certain extent, most leadership roles within an organization fit this description, but some much more than others. Great examples of the player-coach can be found in functional areas: an employee takes on a new role in an organization and brings with them a valuable amount of knowledge or subject matter expertise to their new team. It is often the 'player' skill set that is initially valued, and then at some point in the player's career they may be asked to lead others and they step up to the challenge—becoming a player-coach. They are expected to lead others but also do work related to their subject matter expertise.

Many accomplished leaders started their careers in frontline roles—like customer-service oriented roles—before being promoted to managerial positions and overseeing larger teams of people with equal (or more) knowledge of the function. It was quickly apparent that these individuals were better suited to lead, motivate, and plan, rather than to actually *do* the work. For example, it doesn't take long for a supervisor of ten or more service representatives in a call center to realize there is no way they can answer all of the calls and resolve all of the customers' issues. If this lesson wasn't completely clear after their first promotion, and if they were fortunate enough to get a second promotion, the lesson would intensify as the scope of their role grew to the point that delegating and managing others would eventually be the *only* option to getting work done.

One leader we know who managed the player-coach transition successfully is now a CFO who started his career in financial planning and investor relations. His work effort and individual ability to get things done were what put him on the leadership track, initially as the supervisor of a few other financial types. He recalls the challenges of his early player-coach days: "I was able to stretch and cover all the bases, but my attention to detail and need for perfection led to a total work-life imbalance in my next big promotion. After some self-reflection and awareness, I realized that if I wanted to continue my career growth and I wanted to stay healthy, I had to grow my coaching and leadership skills and lessen my *doing*. My first coach roles were 80 percent doing and 20 percent leading. As I progressed, I got to more of a 50/50 model. Finally, I realized that in the big jobs like I have today, that's just not sustainable." Now as CFO of a billion-dollar retail firm, he describes his role as 80 percent coaching and leading and 20 percent doing. His strategic work today is directly working with the CEO and Board.

Another example of a leader who made a successful player-coach transition is a lawyer whose experience was gained in private practice and on a corporate legal team. While in private practice, her focus was on maximizing hours billed to clients. Her value was exactly measured by what she produced for the client. When she entered the corporate world and eventually led a team of lawyers and paralegals, she began to build and flex different muscles in pursuit of success in her leadership role. "While I remain accountable for my own workload of legal cases, I find myself thinking more and more about my team," she reflects. "I have to remove barriers for them, advocate for them, and think in terms of team effectiveness." She recognized that in some cases she didn't have the right talent in certain roles on her team. "When that happened, I just had to lean in and fill in the lawyer role myself, in an area that was not my strong suit." This player-coach grew from an individual (legal) contributor to an enterprise (legal) leader in the hospitality industry.

A third example of a standout player-coach is a nurse who progressed to become a chief nursing officer in the healthcare industry. Her leadership skills, particularly her ability to deal with people—both leading and collaborating—came fairly naturally to her, so she was given leadership responsibility early in her career. Unlike some player-coaches, she wasn't tempted to micromanage or seek perfection from those she led. In fact, when she was managing the ICU and eighty-plus nurses, she forced herself to stay in touch with the actual work by taking a shift once per month. It was a great example to others and it helped her stay connected with the issues her team faced on a daily basis. She described it as, "A really difficult practice to fit into my schedule, but it was important to my credibility and perspective."

These great leaders successfully transitioned from *doing* to *leading*, but many player-coaches struggle with this concept, and some players never effectively make the transition to coach. They become leaders who are difficult to work for, they do not maximize the potential of those who do work for them, and they often burn themselves out because they are trying to hold on to too much of the scope of work they were doing before their promotion.

There are two interrelated reasons why some player-coaches find the transition more challenging. First, this type of leader knows and understands that their expertise is the value-add that others see. For years, they've been a highly valued subject matter expert, and when they are put into a true player-coach role with expectations of producing their own load as well as 'watching over' others, they may *feel* like their value as a subject matter expert outweighs their ability to lead.

Second, staff or functional leaders struggle because they receive little training or development on how to lead. They certainly get far less training in leadership or people management than they received in their formal, specified education, or in their years of experience in a subject matter.

In his book *Outliers*, Malcolm Gladwell made popular the 10,000-Hour Rule for 'mastery of a task or function.' The original research study by Anders Ericsson demonstrated that it takes approximately 10,000 hours of practice to hone one's skills to a mastery level in any given discipline or role.[2] Since Gladwell's repeated examples in *Outliers*, there have been other studies claiming to debunk the rule. It is not the accuracy of the rule we wish to argue here: we simply want to express that many professionals and subject matter experts spend an enormous number of hours studying and practicing in their careers before they are promoted as people leaders.

Often accountants, lawyers, tax experts, HR professionals, professors, healthcare professionals, and other functional experts have fulfilled or approached 10,000 hours in their education, study, preparation, and practice of a discipline. Others may not have the long-term investment in formal education but may have a unique skill in a function or discipline and are relied on for critical aspects of the function. In both cases, when asked to lead others, they may receive only twenty to twenty-five hours at most of 'manager training,' which is usually limited to administrative tasks and duties rather than the critical aspects of a leadership job, like conflict resolution, how to plan and organize a team, or how to inspire and motivate individuals.

The ratio of a player-coach's subject matter expertise to leadership knowledge, measured by hours of preparation and practice, can easily be 100:1! It is easy to see why a staff leader may feel like their subject matter expertise is more valuable to the organization than their leadership capability. And struggling with the transition from a player/doer to a coach/leader is commonplace, but it can typically be resolved by learning how to balance *doing* with *leading*; and recognize their own value as leaders, not just doers.

We have observed a similar concept exemplified by consultants in the corporate world and put them into two categories: the craftsperson and businessperson. The craftsperson/consultant practiced their craft, was very good at it, and made a living billing for the hours worked. We liked working with the craftspeople: they were reliable, experts in their field, and once they were on-task, you could simply get out of the way and let them run. But their capacity to do work (and certainly their capacity to make money) was limited by the hours in the day—they were the product they sold.

By contrast, the businessperson/consultant usually magnified their impact by bringing in others, creating processes, books, tools, etc., that the customer could use *without the consultant being present*. We liked to say the businessperson made money while they slept. It is this concept of magnifying their impact, expanding their reach through leading others, inspiring others, and allowing them to do the work that is similar to the transition from player/doer to coach/leader. Rather than focusing on the craft at hand, the leader must focus on those who can help in doing the work and increase what can be accomplished by the team.

Why leadership matters

We've all tried to work under an ineffective leader—it's exhausting, frustrating, and can be a reason for leaving the organization. In fact, companies like Gallup, Willis Towers Watson, and Dale Carnegie work with a multitude of firms trying to further understand employee engagement. They all generally agree that people leave *managers*, not *companies*. In short, the central relationship between manager and employee plays a critical role in the employee's overall sense of engagement, and ultimately the success of the company.

Liz Wiseman, author and speaker, uses the term 'multiplier' to describe how a leader increases the capability of others. Wiseman's researched-based view is that an effective leader who delegates, motivates, and inspires actually increases the intelligence of those who work for them and, consequently, multiplies the effectiveness and performance level of those they lead.[3] *And that is what leadership is.* The leader ensures that the team is in place, is aligned, and is stretching to achieve all they can. Being a leader is about more than taking up a spot on the org chart.

Everyone on a team has a role, including the leader. Everyone on the team must be *effective* in their role, including the leader. And if the leader is not effective, it has more of an impact on the entire team than if any other individual member of the team is not effective. The leader must acknowledge the importance of their role, and though they may not master it (remember, mastery is 10,000 hours), they can ensure team effectiveness with effort and focus. If the leader does not play that role well, it is very difficult for anyone else on that team to assume the role, and thus extremely difficult for the team to be successful. That is why it is so critical that the player-coach recognize the importance of balancing their coach/leader role with their player/doer role.

A player-coach success model

We have talked about balancing the coach/leader role and the player/doer role, but what exactly is the coach/leader role and what does it mean to succeed at it? Our player-coach success model highlights the four aspects that are critical for the player-coach if the team is to be effective:

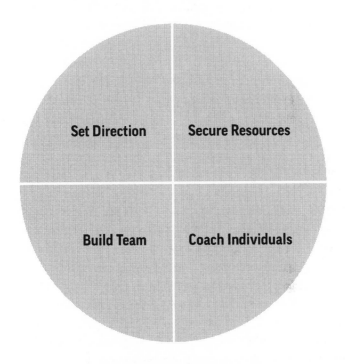

A PLAYER-COACH SUCCESS MODEL

Before we dive into each aspect of this model in Part Two, we want to share some advice from one of the great people leaders we have worked with. He always taught this critical lesson to player-coaches who worked in his organization (those leaders he promoted into their roles): in order to effectively play their role, the player-coach must first *do what only they can do*. Read this carefully. A player-coach focuses first on *the duties that are theirs and can't be done by others*. Things like establishing the direction of the team or organization, ensuring that the team or organization is properly resourced, aligning and motivating the team, addressing any performance or staffing issues, removing roadblocks that only they can, and guiding the development and growth of the team and individuals on the team.

If a player-coach can remember to apply this one principle, they will have a greater likelihood of being successful. But it is also important to understand what this principle is *not* saying: it is not saying that player-coaches *do the things they are the best* at or that are important for the team to get right. A player-coach may have to be more heavily involved in, or even have to do some of those tasks, but their primary role is to *not do everything themselves*. Their primary role is to ensure that their team has all of the necessary resources and is functional and capable of operating with a high-level of efficiency. By focusing solely on the tasks that highlight what they are 'best at,' a player-coach will miss huge opportunities to develop the team and increase their performance.

Now that we've set the stage for the model, let's dig deeper into each aspect and the elements and actions that support them. Chapters 2 through 5 focus on the four segments of the model. The model and its elements are not linear, although some elements must naturally precede others. Likewise, a player-coach does not have to focus on all four aspects equally. Numerous factors affect how and when a player-coach should focus their time and energy, and as we move through the book we will point out reasons and situations that may demand focus on one area more than others.

"Here's something they'll probably
never teach you in business school.
**The single biggest decision you make in
your job—bigger than all the rest—is who
you name manager. When you name
the wrong person manager, nothing fixes
that bad decision. Not compensation,
not benefits—nothing."**

JIM CLIFTON, IN THE SUMMARY ACCOMPANYING
GALLUP'S 2013 STATE OF THE AMERICAN
WORKPLACE EMPLOYEE ENGAGEMENT STUDY[4]

PART

A PLAYER-COACH SUCCESS MODEL

TWO

Player-coaches often complain when staff do not meet their expectations, and that they find it easier to 'do it themselves.' It may be easier in the short-term for the player-coach to perform the task themselves instead of taking the time to coach and force the 'redoing' to the one who should be doing it. But as long as the player-coach does the task, the person who should be doing it does not learn or understand what is to be done.

2

SET DIRECTION

"OF ALL THE attributes my leader possesses, what I appreciate most is her ability to paint the vision and direction of where we are going and articulate it in a way that we all want to get there. She seems to see where things are headed and is always a step or two ahead. The way she focuses and connects everything we do to the mission of our larger organization makes us all want to follow her. She sets the bar high. Sometimes it is difficult to imagine we can get there, but we do not want to disappoint her. She is constantly reminding us of our mission and the value we bring to those we serve."

A DIRECT REPORT REGARDING THEIR LEADER
IN THE HEALTHCARE INDUSTRY

Set Direction

- Understand expectations
- Make plans
- Prioritize
- Set objectives and expectations
- Communicate for alignment
- Reflect and adjust
- Create a vision for the future

Secure Resources

Build Team

Coach Individuals

TEAM LEADERS ARE responsible for setting direction and ensuring that their team's actions support that direction: they do not necessarily have to determine exactly where the team is going and the route they will take to get there alone. Often, effective leaders will involve their team when gathering information or exploring scenarios to identify direction. It is the leader's responsibility to set the final direction and to ensure all team members are on board.

Player-coaches must prioritize setting their team's direction, planning, communicating the plans to their team, and ensuring their team is aligned to those plans. They should also monitor, reflect, and adjust the plans as needed for their team to be successful. Setting direction includes the following aspects:

Understand expectations

First off, the player-coach must understand the organization's expectations for the team: what is required for the team to succeed. The process of establishing a good understanding of expectations is likely to be highly iterative.

The player-coach's supervisor is the best resource for written documents like job descriptions, department guidelines, and customer-supplier documents, which are key sources of information when establishing expectations. Team members can also help by offering personal insight and describing their objectives.

In some professions, it's important to understand what rules apply to how people work, and any laws that may influence or dictate actions people may take regarding work. For instance, in the world of accounting, employers and employees must follow the guidelines established by the Federal Accounting Standards Advisory Board (FASAB). In healthcare and human resources professions, the Health Insurance Portability and Accountability Act (HIPAA) is an important part of exchanging information; and the Occupational Safety and Health Administration (OSHA) sets the standards for how safety and health is conducted in the workplace.

It can also be helpful to seek critical information from those who possess specific knowledge and who have organizational influence. A great example of this comes from the technology space, where a colleague of ours (also a newly appointed leader), Ron, was identified to head up a product and service rollout beyond the pilot phase. He requested a meeting with the CFO to gain a better understanding of how this service actually made money: how the costs were distributed, what the business case was for developing the service, how the organization had priced the service, what customer acquisition costs were, and how success would be measured.

Ron spent two days with the CFO immersing himself in the details of the service and how it related to the expectations—especially the financial expectations—that he was to meet. He still had more to learn regarding the service rollout, but this investment gave him a greater understanding of the financial expectations for his and his team's work, and how to start planning.

Make plans

Once a player-coach clearly understands the expectations for their team, they must make plans for the team to meet these expectations on an ongoing basis. It is good practice to include the team in planning, because their experience and expertise on 'how' to meet expectations will provide helpful insight.

Planning documents should define the team's expectations, how they will be achieved, and how the team will interface with each other and to other parts of the organization that are critical to the team's ability to meet its goals. Chapter 6 (page 127) provides more tips about organizing and planning.

Prioritize

In most organizations, the workload exceeds the available resources, and there are always more opportunities to chase than we can catch or successfully handle. One of the critical roles of the player-coach is to prioritize and ensure the team understands, and is aligned to, the priorities.

Often, the player-coach will want to get many things going within the team, and as new ideas are generated, they will want to put the ideas into action. The player-coach may be an idea generator or may be responding to requests of others, but it is easy to put more in the hopper than the team can actually accomplish. The effective player-coach will recognize the capacity of the team, motivate them to surpass their goals, but ensure they don't burn out or become frustrated if they can't accomplish everything.

One of the best leaders we ever worked with was a master at articulating fewer priorities than the number of digits on one hand and describing those priorities whenever he addressed individuals in the organization. Everyone knew the organization's three to five priorities in any given year. Every town hall meeting, every letter to employees, every podcast began with "Let's talk about how we are doing on our priorities."

It was thrilling to see what the organization could do when everyone was focused. Not only did this leader talk about the priorities, he made sure they were ever-present in the workplace: on banners and posters in hallways, on every web page, and as part of his presentations to the executive team and to the Board. This type of discipline, when pushed throughout the organization, can result in great progress on priorities.

Ensuring priorities are set and understood is a key task that only a player-coach can do for the organization. This doesn't mean the player-coach has to prioritize in a vacuum—they can involve the team and others in the organization—but the player-coach is the one responsible for ensuring that the team owns the priorities, and for reinforcing them.

Invariably, once priorities are set and the team is aligned to them, something will come up that is outside of, beyond, or unconnected to those priorities. And priorities will shift slightly as the organization or its leaders shift their attention. In this case, the player-coach must analyze, adjust, and determine how the team should respond. There are times when plans and priorities have to shift, and this helps teams determine how adaptable they are. Changes in plans and priorities are a positive learning event and can help teams and coaches flex their prioritization muscles.

Set objectives and expectations

Every player-coach is responsible for setting the tone for their team, meaning they should work hard to set objectives and expectations that will keep the team on track and help individuals learn how they contribute to the organization's success. Setting direction is not just about following direction.

Setting objectives and expectations includes defining a set of values for how people work together. These statements or beliefs are often set at the company level and can help the team understand the difference between right and wrong. They can also be the guardrails that the team abides by as they work.

There are many ways a player-coach can focus on setting the appropriate tone for the team. One player-coach's personality may lend itself to creating a buzz for the organization by developing a slogan that motivates the team toward a goal. Another player-coach may choose to focus on their own behavior by setting an example of how they want the team to operate: if a player-coach expects people to be on time or early to meetings, then *they should be on time or early to meetings*. This same premise is displayed by the player-coach's priorities: if a player-coach spends the first hour of every day on the computer and not with the team, they will see that choice as the priority. One note of caution: while leading by example is table stakes, the player-coach still has to communicate expectations and match those expectations with action. Otherwise, you may be setting an example with no one watching.

Communicate for alignment

The player-coach who works hard to communicate and align work to goals will earn the respect of their team over time. Timely, effective, authentic communications keep teams in the know about what is essential for them to succeed. By aligning individual team members to the overall goal, everyone clearly understands the requirements, and why said requirements are what they are.

When assigning work, the player-coach must clearly explain the *what* and the *why* of the situation. Often team members will consider assigned work to be 'normal business,' i.e, part of the overall goals and objectives of the team. However, there are times when the team may not understand a shift in direction, or the player-coach may not be able to shift the team without upsetting their priorities. Before a player-coach simply passes new work on to their team, the team needs to understand what's going on, which could mean a pointed discussion about why the shift has occurred, and the implications on existing projects and priorities.

The player-coach's role is not to simply *pass on* the message from above in the organization, but to understand the message and its implications. They must have the courage to *push* the message back uphill for clarification, and to help those above understand the impacts of the shift on existing work. This may not result in a reversal of the shift, but the player-coach will be better prepared to direct their team on how to handle the change, and then to reprioritize and figure out what work to displace, slow down, or move to the back burner. That is the player-coach's job.

Reflect and adjust

Over time, player-coaches will finesse the way they step back, observe the team's work, reflect on progress, and adjust the objectives and expectations. This observation should not be intrusive or overly inspective: simply asking questions to understand how and why individuals or small groups choose to perform work is a good way for a player-coach to engage.

From the get-go it is essential for the player-coach to consistently set aside time to reflect on the team's progress, and to consider how they want to influence and positively change the work environment and the team's direction to ensure continued success. When a player-coach adjusts a plan with the best interest of the team in mind, and clearly communicates it, it is a sign of strength and engagement.

Create a vision for the future

Great player-coaches will always have a vision of where the team or organization can go. Many believe the 'vision' thing is reserved for the CEO or the founder/entrepreneur who inspires the whole organization to follow them, but we believe that vision should be on the agenda at every level of leadership. A good player-coach helps their team see the larger strategic direction and the role they play within the greater good of the organization, the community, or the world.

As the player-coach progresses in their role, they should think about how the team can add more value to the larger organization. By including the team in the process, the player-coach can create a vision for the future that bolsters the ongoing objectives and expectations.

Ideally the visioning process should include a discussion about team performance standards. Here are some examples of questions that will solicit the team's collective ideas (input) and unify the resulting team vision (the output):

- What does success mean to us?
- How do we live up to our values and goals?
- Why do we care about getting our job done?
- How do we see success with our partners, suppliers, and customers?

We have coached hundreds of people in our careers and are confident that the ability to create a vision for the future is a skill that any coach or leader can develop over time. Coaches and leaders will become more confident in creating a vision the more often they do it. Remember that the future—both immediate and long-term—is unknown, so the skill of creating a tangible connection to an unseen, unrealized goal is what the player-coach should focus on. As player-coaches establish and cultivate a vision for the future, that vision should have strong purpose, be ambitious, and not limited to what is perceived to be possible today.

"The reason most people never reach their goals is that they don't define them, or ever seriously consider them as believable or achievable. Winners can tell you where they are going, what they plan to do along the way, and who will be sharing the adventure with them."

DENIS WAITLEY,
WRITER AND MOTIVATIONAL SPEAKER[5]

3

SECURE
RESOURCES

"WHEN I CAME into the role I knew the objective was to take the company public, and the finance function was a critical capability to do that. When I completed an evaluation of what we had and what we needed, I realized how far we were from being able to meet that goal. We lacked people, processes, and tools—and all that costs money. I laid out an extremely aggressive plan along with the investment I thought we needed and presented it to leadership. They backed the plan and we got to work. We purchased the software we needed, upgraded tools, and put in processes and systems. We brought in new skills and talent. When I look back at it now, it was a very difficult journey, but the very successful public offering achieved a few years back and our continued success show it was well worth it."

FIRST-TIME CFO OF A SMALL RETAIL BUSINESS
THAT SUCCESSFULLY WENT PUBLIC

Secure Resources

- Identify resource requirements
- Assess existing resources
- Identify interdependencies
- Acquire funding and other resources
- Put talent in the best places
- Constantly remove roadblocks

Set Direction

Build Team

Coach Individuals

HAVE YOU EVER been in a job where you were asked to excel without access to the resources that you knew would make the job easier, the product more accurate, and the process much smoother? If you have, you know how frustrating it can be. A Gallup research study found that one of the key predictors of employee engagement and productivity was the response to the statement, "I have the equipment and materials I need to do my job right."[6]

A critical role for the player-coach is to secure the resources—the talent, equipment, training, information, and support—that the team needs to fulfill its commitments to the organization and to achieve its goals. To do this, the player-coach has the following key tasks:

Identify resource requirements

Whether during one-on-one discussions with team members, or part of ongoing staff meetings, the player-coach should stay on top of resource requirements. This not only sets a good leadership tone, but also helps to ensure that the team has the tools for success. Some things like supplies and equipment may be obvious, but other resource requirements, like specific training or upgraded software, may be less so. People are resources too, so the player-coach should also make sure to listen to ideas about allocating people resources from those actually doing the work.

While presenting the player-coach success model at a leadership development session recently, we asked participants about the effective techniques they had used to identify and secure resources for their team. A player-coach from a communications company shared this experience:

> In a team meeting with my direct reports, I was asked how much our training budget was. I floundered somewhat in my response, because I honestly didn't know the answer. I told the team I would get back to them on 'how much,' and I also asked what brought the question on. Several people said they wanted to nurture their professional development: grow their own skill set, and also expand their knowledge and experience in other areas of the company. They had witnessed colleagues going to various events and training, and they were just curious as to how they could participate in similar activities.
>
> In my next one-on-one with my manager, I inquired about the training budget. She turned the question on me and said, "How much do you need?" Again, I floundered because I couldn't answer the question. I shared my previous experience with her and she graciously advised me to develop a plan for what I needed, and we would discuss it.
>
> I went back to the team and asked them to give me their wish list for training. Not knowing what kind feedback to expect, I encouraged them to approach the list similarly to how they (or their kids) might write a list for Santa: sometimes you want one or two big things, and sometimes you just want a lot of great stocking stuffers! To my surprise the team actually met on their own and opted to make their Santa lists individually and then regroup and consolidate their wishes—many of which ended up being

similar—and then they presented the list to me. I was truly proud of their diligence and hard work.

When I shared the list with my manager at our next one-on-one, she took the time to walk through it with me and we found that our company provided most of the training that was requested in-house or online. The remainder of the wishes were conferences. We then determined who would go to which conference, and the team members who went were to 'teach or share' their learnings with the whole team.

A player-coach can gain great credibility with their team by identifying and resolving any frustrations caused by poor equipment, inadequate supplies, or other insufficient resources. We often coach leaders who step into new roles to look for resource issues they can champion for their team because it helps gain the team's trust and lets the team know the leader is *for* them. Reducing one or more of the pain points caused by inadequate equipment, information, or other resources can start a new leader off on the right foot with their team. This is one of the responsibilities that, likely, only the leader can fulfill.

Assess existing resources

The player-coach should periodically assess the state of existing resources by defining those resources that are 'must haves' to accomplish the team's goals and objectives and identifying any gaps. Once a list is produced it can be modified over time. This exercise can help a player-coach think about whether the team is bumping along with what it has, or if it is well positioned for current and future success. If there are any gaps, the player-coach should develop an action plan to secure the right resources over time.

Assessing a team's existing resources includes determining the equipment, technology, information, and other physical assets needed to succeed. It also includes assessing the *human resources* and evaluating whether or not the team possesses the talent and skill set to operate successfully. Does the team have enough people to meet expectations? Are the current team members in the right roles, and do they have the correct skills to do the job?

The opening quote in this chapter is a great example of a player-coach assessing—and then securing—the resources his team needed to excel. This same CFO told us that when he arrived in his role, much of the monthly revenue and expense reports were assembled and calculated by hand: dozens of hours of individual work by multiple employees went into each report. The CFO knew that system would not fly for a publicly traded company, so he put together a business case for the CEO on what was needed to make this process more efficient. He knew that the skills needed to manage new systems and processes would be different from the skills required to do manual calculations and reports, so he included both training and talent acquisition in his business plan.

While some members of the company's leadership group thought his proposal for both software investments and people investments were far beyond what was needed—they had done just fine with what they had for years, thank you very much!—the CFO was able to persuade leadership to make the investment and provide the resources he asked for.

Identify interdependencies

Within many organizations, some teams rely on other teams for information or to perform part of a process to deliver products or services. If a company is manufacturing a product, for example, one team might focus on a single component of the product, and another team on different component. A third team might be waiting on both components in order to assemble the final product. These situations create interdependencies among the teams.

When securing resources for their team, the player-coach must consider these kinds of interdependencies while keeping the big picture in mind. It may well be the case that, for the total process to improve, the resources that the player-coach manages are needed elsewhere in the organization or are equally needed across the entire process.

Patrick Lencioni, author of *The Five Dysfunctions of a Team*, introduces the concept that each member of a team should be willing to sacrifice in order for the team to succeed.[7] The objective is not necessarily for one function or one team to be the best in their discipline, but for that function or team to be the best at what the company needs it to do to be the best overall. The successful leader will recognize and work within this tradeoff when seeking resources for the team.

Acquire funding and other resources

One critical 'resource' for a team is funding, and it is the player-coach's job to secure it. Most organizations do not have limitless budgets to meet every need, so the role of the player-coach may be to persuade decision-makers, to do extensive research, and/or build a business case (who, what, when, where, how, and why) to secure the funding they want.

To build successful and compelling arguments, the player-coach must learn to respond to questions like, "Why should we fund this? Describe the increased productivity or product enhancements that will be generated by the company if we decide to invest in your idea. What is the value proposition for investing in new technology?"

Sometimes the request or ideas are not well received, or it is not comfortable or easy to obtain what is needed, but acquiring funding is a role that only the leader of the team can fulfill.

DEVELOPING A BUSINESS CASE: GETTING TO 'YES'

I'LL NEVER FORGET the sinking feeling I had early in my career when my manager said, "Build me a business case and I'll take it to my boss." I had asked for more staff and equipment to handle the work demand, and I didn't even know what a 'business case' was. Not wanting to admit that, I simply said, "Will do," and left my manager's office.

After dealing with my frustration, I did the two things I knew to do at the time: I asked my peers and a few other trusted souls in the department if they had examples of effective business cases they could share; and I made a list of questions I would ask myself if I were making a big purchase like a car or house.

I learned two things from this experience: first, there was no single 'right' template for a business case, as all of my colleagues' examples were different; and second, I knew how to come up with good questions that helped me design an effective business case.

Throughout my career, I've had multiple opportunities to develop and present business cases of varying kinds. I still rely on those two key lessons: let the opportunity dictate the structure of the business case itself; and develop a set of questions that likely need to be answered before you can get to 'yes.' Sharing a draft business case with colleagues prior to submitting or presenting it also helps you tighten your case and prepare for potential questions and arguments.

TAMMY

Put talent in the best places

The balance of people and talent who make up a team are key factors to its success. It is the player-coach's role to answer the following questions:

- Is the team the right size?
- Does the team have the talent and skills needed to do the job successfully?
- Are people in the right roles on the team so we can leverage the talent that exists?

Sometimes these decisions are clear and easily made, and sometimes they are not. But this is the foremost role of the player-coach: to ensure the right people are situated in the right roles in the team at the right time.

In his book *Good to Great: Why Some Companies Make the Leap... and Other's Don't*, Jim Collins talks about the concept of 'first who, then what.'[8] This involves getting the most out of each person on the team as well as recognizing when 'the most out of the person' is not enough to succeed. We have worked with very good player-coaches who are great at the first but may not recognize that, while they are getting the best out of their team, the team is still not capable of achieving their objectives.

Getting the right people into the right roles can be a challenging endeavor, especially when the player-coach knows that they don't have the right talent on the team to be effective. This may be because the team was asked to take on new roles or assignments, or because the player-coach was asked to take on a new team. In either case, the player-coach must determine how many people are needed and what skills and talents they require. The player-coach must also determine how they can build (train, develop) or buy (hire, select) the talent needed.

The most difficult decisions here are usually about those who are not in the right roles, or even on the right team. All too often these issues go on for years without being addressed properly. We have seen player-coaches deal with the problem by simply picking up more work themselves while allowing the misplaced person to continue, but this means the player-coach will be less effective in their coach role, and it allows a resource to be somewhat 'wasted.' The player-coach must address the issue by doing what needs to be done in a respectful way, and with consideration for all individuals involved. This is the work of leadership, and unless the player-coach performs this role effectively, the whole team will struggle.

GREAT PERSON, WRONG JOB

ABOUT TWO-THIRDS OF the way through my career, I took on a new assignment. The role was familiar to me, as I had done it a little earlier in my career for a different organization, but in this case, it was with an inherited team—all of the team members had been chosen by my predecessor.

After about thirty days in the role, I knew one of my direct reports—let's call her Joan—was not the right person for her current job. I had to think this through before acting: Joan was highly respected, was great at the career she had been in for fifteen years, and had been recently placed in a 'stretch' assignment so she could grow her strategic skills. Joan's career prior to that point had been in operations in a highly structured environment, where outcomes of doing her job effectively were evident every day. In her stretch assignment the work environment was highly creative, and the outcomes could take years to mature.

I told myself that I was going to support the stretch assignment, give honest, constructive feedback, and help Joan to succeed in six months. I supported all the right things: 360-degree feedback, executive learning experiences, access to more resources with knowledge and background in the discipline— you name it. Nothing worked. After six months I was exhausted, Joan was exhausted. Feeling defeated, I went to my boss to gain support for putting Joan back in a role where she could be successful.

Together, my boss and I worked every angle we could to find an entry point for Joan back into operations. After what seemed to be forever, there still were no opportunities. In a discussion I had with Joan, she asked if she could try looking herself. I said,

"Sure!" Within thirty days, Joan had a plan, a role, and an opportunity that she was excited about.

What did I learn? That people who are great contributors but might be in the wrong job will generally recognize the situation and be more motivated to find (and own) their next step than you are.

TAMMY

As coach/leaders who assume responsibility for a new team, we start evaluating the team and each individual team member on day one of the new assignment. It may take some time to determine whether the team has the right members in the right roles, but the process should start immediately.

Part of the responsibility of positioning talent in the right places is to ensure that the right people are brought into the organization. The way candidates are identified and screened can be critical to finding the right person for a particular role. We would like to highlight a couple of points about 'talent selection.'

First, while people usually select an individual for a specific role, taking a longer-term perspective and considering what the person's next move might be, or where else they could serve the organization, is instrumental in securing talent for the long haul. In other words, leaders should play chess in their people-selection rather than checkers. Sometimes this isn't feasible: a certain function may need critical expertise and cannot do without it, which is understandable. However, whenever it *is* feasible, playing chess in people-selection will pay off in the long run.

Team chemistry, or the bonds and working relationships among the people within a group, is also an important consideration in talent selection. Chemistry is a huge contributing factor in the results of a team, particularly as the business world relies more on technology and a collaborative workforce.

The importance of chemistry is directly proportional to the interdependence or interconnections within the team. If the individuals in the team or group have completely different and independent functions from one another, chemistry may not be as critical. But if members of a team hand parts of the process off to one another, or depend highly on one another, chemistry can make or break the team's success.

When the player-coach is hiring or selecting for a highly interdependent team, we recommend that they ask current team members to participate when interviewing candidates. This gives both the candidate and the team members a chance to interact and connect. After the interview, the player-coach should ask existing team members questions like, "Do you want to work with this person? What are the positive takeaways you have? Did anything concern you?" It may not always be possible to select the candidate that the team wants—or that every member of the team wants—but the player-coach with a highly interdependent team should pay close attention to their responses to those questions.

Constantly remove roadblocks

The last critical component of the player-coach's role in securing resources is removing roadblocks that are hampering the team from achieving its goals—no matter how small or how daunting the task may be. Roadblocks can be internal or external to the team and/or the company. Internal roadblocks are things like other team members, policies, procedures, or management practices that cause conflicts in getting work done successfully. External factors could be vendors/suppliers or even the end customer.

For some player-coaches, removing roadblocks is a real challenge because it often requires dealing with conflict or confronting colleagues and others who are blocking (intentionally or unintentionally) the team's progress. Sometimes it means 'challenging up' the leadership above you to help decision-makers understand what it will take to achieve what they have asked of the team. Other times it requires meeting with a colleague or a partner who may not understand or want the team to do what they have been asked to do. It may mean advocating for a reasonable exception to a policy so that progress can be made more quickly, or tackling a myriad of other things curtailing a team's progress.

The work of removing roadblocks does not mean the player-coach simply receives the problems of the team and challenges up or across to solve the problems. The player-coach must first establish whether or not the team can resolve the problem internally before looking for solutions outside the team.

Activities to remove roadblocks usually have one thing in common: they require a player-coach to challenge or confront a person or a group on behalf of their team. This can be uncomfortable, but this is the player-coach's role. It is one of those things that only the player-coach can do, and it is often critical for a team to progress. Nothing will cement a player-coach's credibility and their team's trust in them more than a leader who advocates for them and their work.

"If you have the wrong people, **it doesn't matter whether you discover the right direction; you still won't have a great company. Great vision without great people is irrelevant.**"

JIM COLLINS, AUTHOR OF *GOOD TO GREAT*[9]

4

COACH
INDIVIDUALS

"SHE SUPPORTS HER people, provides guidance, and involves her people. She is not afraid of letting her direct reports take the ball and run with it. When they veer off course, she allows them to feel the pain and then course corrects. She advocates for us and talks about the work we are doing. She gives you credit for the work you are doing. She doesn't simply take your work and make the presentation. She provides exposure to those below her. She leads without being too directive. She values my being closer to the work. She is consistent—same as she was when we were peers, but I am now seeing she is also a leader who is a thought partner. She addresses performance issues head-on. First leader I have had to really address them."

MULTIPLE COMMENTS FROM A WORK TEAM ABOUT
THEIR LEADER IN A HOSPITALITY COMPANY

Set Direction

Secure Resources

Build Team

Coach Individuals
- Observe and learn
- Listen and understand
- Coach and develop
- Give ongoing feedback
- Hold individuals accountable
- Stretch and motivate

LET'S THINK ABOUT the term 'coach.' It means to train, instruct, prompt, urge, or direct someone with instructions. We believe a coach at work is part teacher, part encourager, and part role model.

There are six attributes to coaching that, when used together, create a remarkable coaching experience for the individual—an experience where growth *and* success are present.

The length of this chapter relative to others reflects just how important coaching individuals is to the player-coach role compared to all other aspects of leadership.

Observe and learn

Good player-coaches have a sense of what their team members are producing and how their team members are doing. To achieve that understanding, a player-coach must observe their team members and learn how they work and who they are.

Player-coaches assist those they lead; they guide them in the direction most beneficial to the person and the organization. To do this effectively, the player-coach must *know them* (know the person and the professional, know their capabilities and their deficiencies) and *observe them* (see how they perform their work). Without this information, the player-coach is really impeded in their ability to assist or direct.

A player-coach should observe their team when they can, and seek to understand the progress and challenges of those they lead. Player-coaches should know when those they lead are:

- doing a good job and only need some support and encouragement;
- struggling and need assistance;
- out of alignment with the group and need some course correction; or
- failing, and more drastic measures are called for.

In Chapter 6 (page 99), we discuss observation skills and tactics in detail.

While observation is necessary to be an effective leader, it is insufficient without action. Whether observations are gathered in person or through feedback loops and processes, the information is of no use unless it is acted upon—for example, by coaching, praising, or even disciplining the individual.

Listen and understand

Listening is an important aspect of coaching because it enables a player-coach to connect with the individual coachee. Listening and understanding are essential components to healthy communication, and a foundation for trust. When individuals feel they are being heard, they will more openly share their ideas and provide honest feedback. Conversely, an employee who feels that their boss doesn't have time, or take time, to talk with them, or that their opinions are not valued, will likely experience issues with engagement and morale.

Player-coaches, like all leaders, are pulled in many directions, but it's crucial to make time to listen to employees and understand their input about work. In Chapter 6 (page 103), we offer tips for how player-coaches can develop the critical skill of active listening.

Coach and develop

The team leader is a key influencer in the professional development of their team members, and it is their job to define or identify what development looks like for each individual. This could be different from one person to the next, or the same for the entire team.

We often ask groups, "What is the first thing that comes to mind when we say 'employee development'?" Invariably, the most common answer is, "Training." But the good player-coach recognizes that development has little to do with training, and views development from a very different lens.

To shift the thinking about development from training, we like to use what has become known as the 70-20-10 Model for Learning and Development. This principle states that 70 percent of development is experience—either on the job or off the job. Another 20 percent is relationships—coaching, mentoring, supervisor feedback, peer feedback, etc. Only 10 percent of development is classroom training or education.

The 70-20-10 Model is generally considered to have its roots in the research conducted by Morgan McCall Jr., Michael Lombardo, and Ann Morrison from the Center for Creative Leadership (CCL).[10] The culmination of their research is a book entitled *The Lessons of Experience: How Successful Executives Develop on the Job.*[11] It was first published in 1988 and we still consider it the seminal work on executive development. McCall, Lombardo, and Morrison interviewed almost a thousand executives seeking to understand what they considered their most meaningful development. The overwhelming conclusion from the research was that people develop through experience much more than by formal education. They then identified a host of situations based on their research that they considered major development experiences, including those like the following.

Dramatic increase in scope. A dramatic increase in scope can take on many different forms: doubling the size of one's workforce, expanding sales territory or footprint, or being asked to lead multiple disciplines are a few examples. When asked to take on significantly more responsibility, people can be energized by the idea and the opportunity, they can be overwhelmed—or a little bit of both. The positive energy that comes from being entrusted with a greater scope of responsibilities will generally increase the speed and effectiveness of a leader's decisions. An increase in scope requires a leader to rethink approaches to planning, time management, and communication, which will in turn contribute to their development.

Starting an operation from scratch. Starting something from scratch can be an excellent growth experience because it gives someone the opportunity to create and act without a complete procedural manual—and even sometimes without a boss breathing down their neck. It also often requires someone to wear many hats until they grow the operation enough to divide it into different functions. The CCL research cited examples such as starting major manufacturing plants or new stores, but start-ups don't necessarily have to be grandiose to help one gain confidence that they can create something. Development can come from doing something as modest as creating a policy or a different procedure for handling something in the office or group.

Stepping into a difficult situation. When stepping into a difficult situation where performance is low and a turnaround is expected, the common response is to think that there's no place to go but up! To meet the expectation of quick and significant improvement requires a combination of showing the organization a clear path forward, motivating and inspiring people to succeed, and making tough decisions about people—all of which are developmental experiences that will help the leader grow.

Going through a hardship. Hardships can't be built into a development plan, but they can build character and be of great value developmentally. Pivotal life moments like missing out on a promotion, being demoted or let go, or losing a loved one don't usually feel beneficial at the time, but many people identify these types of hardships as beneficial when looking back at the experience. A player-coach can help those they lead to see the silver lining of hardships, and to move forward with greater purpose.

These are just a few of an infinite number of potential developmental experiences. The player-coach can be creative and proactive in identifying those that will work best for their individual team members.

Exposure to executives and decision-makers can also be very meaningful in shaping and influencing someone's professional development. Here are some simple ideas for creating exposure opportunities:

- When a team member contributes to a presentation that a player-coach must give, they could be invited to observe the player-coach's presentation, or even better, asked to share in the presenting.

- When an executive who has had limited interface with the team visits the team's work area, the player-coach should introduce the executive to the team and find a way for the executive and staff to have a two-way discussion.
- If, in the player-coach's absence, someone must represent the group, the assignment could be given to someone as a development opportunity.
- The player-coach could ask a team member to be a liaison or alliance partner with another organization to bring a broader perspective to the team.

As these ideas suggest, we believe that the most valuable development happens in ways other than sitting in a classroom or formal training: it is the *doing* that helps us grow. Even what we learn in a classroom is not really complete without applying the learning outside the classroom, adapting it as we experiment with it, and internalizing the lesson to be our own (by the way, *perspective* can be impacted greatly in the classroom).

The value of *experience* in regard to people's growth and development can't be stressed enough. In fact, we believe the weighting in the 70-20-10 Model should be even more lopsided in favor of experience. Experience plays a huge and unparalleled role in our growth and development, and the wise player-coach will understand that training and education are necessary but not sufficient, and team members need opportunities and experiences that will help them grow. On the surface, it seems simple. Some player-coaches may say, "You want to grow? Then get back to work." But it is not that simple. It takes thought, planning, and prioritization by the player-coach to assist in the growth of those they lead.

We often refer to a 'steep learning curve' when there is a lot to learn or if something is challenging, but as the graph depicts,

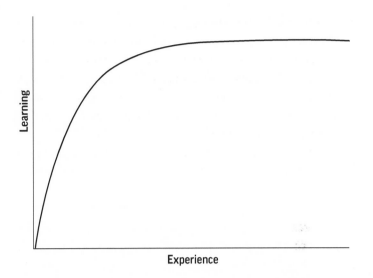

a steep curve implies rapid learning for a relatively short period of time. In terms of development, a steep learning curve is a good thing.

Typically, first-time assignments represent steep learning curves. However, with second-time assignments there is less of a learning curve and more of an opportunity to make an impact. The player-coach who looks only to maximize performance rarely gives someone an opportunity for a first-time assignment. They are more focused on ensuring the work is done efficiently and effectively. That is not a bad thing from a team performance perspective, but this kind of leadership doesn't support individual growth: first-time assignments are the growth engines for individuals. In fact, if someone is asked to do something they have done three or four times before, they likely will do very well, but they are not likely to gain much from the experience. It is the challenge of a new and different assignment that encourages growth.

Give ongoing feedback

The player-coach must foster a feedback culture to ensure individual growth. A once- or twice-yearly review where all actions and behaviors are synthesized and evaluated is not enough to promote a feedback culture. A culture of feedback means that real-time input and suggestions are given on an ongoing basis. Each day, as a player-coach observes individuals on the team, they offer team members positive reinforcement for what they are doing well, and constructive suggestions on what they could do better.

The purpose of coaching is to help others grow and improve. Everyone has the capacity to grow and improve, no matter how long they have been part of an organization, part of a team, or in a specific job. But let's face it: giving feedback is tough, and many of us grew up with the mindset of 'if you have nothing good to say, say nothing at all.' But if a player-coach talks only about the positive outcomes, the team and individual team members will likely not meet business goals.

Kim Scott articulates the ideal balance to strive for with feedback in her book *Radical Candor: Be a Kick-Ass Boss without Losing Your Humanity*.[12] Scott employs a two-dimensional model for effective feedback: the first dimension is the care you show for the person with whom you are working, the second is the directness or candor you use in providing feedback. To summarize the major theme of the book: you must show care and concern to those you lead and, having established that you care for them, you must also have the courage to speak the truth to them.

It is sometimes difficult for people to accept constructive criticism, so a player-coach needs to show positive regard. How do we show positive regard? First, by simply expressing it with statements such as, "Good job on the presentation today.

I like the way you [blank]." "I'm glad you are on our team." "I have seen how hard you have been working and want to thank you." A player-coach can also show positive regard with mindful actions, like remembering important dates, or noticing when things are tough for a team member or when they might need a little boost. Positive regard is important, because rarely are we completely skilled and superbly effective with our feedback.

To be effective, feedback should have three characteristics. It should be direct enough to be heard and understood; specific enough to pinpoint what is to be addressed; and it should be actionable and enable someone to change their behavior going forward. Let's look at these one at a time.

Directness. When a message has to be delivered, it should be *delivered*. Feedback should be direct enough that the person receiving it understands the message; they should not have to guess what the player-coach is saying or asking them to do.

'Direct' means clear and objective; it does *not* mean cruel, revengeful, or hurtful. That said, some feedback can't be sugarcoated. In our corporate careers, we knew a very capable colleague who was both direct *and* brutal in giving feedback. The feedback was generally spot on, although may have been delivered in a direct and dramatic fashion for effect. When people received feedback from this leader, it was clear they had been hit with it—we know, because we received her feedback ourselves. It was not a fun experience.

Although the effectiveness of her approach was debatable, we came away from our interactions with this leader thinking that her words had been important for us to hear. We may have chosen to receive it more tactfully, but we could not reject her message because of the delivery. In fact, we cultivated that relationship because we knew she would have the courage to give us feedback that we may not have received otherwise. It was a bit like going to the dentist for a root canal—we braced ourselves and prepared for an uncomfortable few hours, but we knew the pain was worth hearing the unvarnished truth.

A 360-degree feedback process is another way to promote direct feedback, only in this case it is anonymous. Anonymous feedback is gathered from all directions (peers, direct reports, leaders, etc.) through an online tool or through a third party in an interview setting.

See Chapter 6 for more practical tips on delivering feedback to team members.

Specificity. Feedback must be specific so that the person receiving it knows precisely what it refers to and what actions or behaviors are being discussed. It is not enough for the player-coach to say, "I didn't like it," or, "That went poorly." What is it that the player-coach didn't like or why did it go poorly? Non-specific feedback only causes damage without a path to turn it around.

Specificity could describe behavior, like how the person made the presentation (e.g., looked more at the slides than at the audience). It could include the work product (e.g., the statistics in the report or presentation were not accurate), or the attitude (e.g., the person seemed really defensive when responding to questions regarding the project). The point is that the person receiving the feedback has to have enough information to know *what* is being described.

THE THREE MAGIC QUESTIONS

LATE IN MY career, I stumbled on some advice at a conference that I took away and made my own practice. Somehow without even trying, this routine then spread like wildfire throughout my entire organization—a sign that there must be some magic in this simple practice.

Regardless of the performance policy that exists in a company—formal or informal, prescribed, designed tools, or none at all—feedback sessions should be forthright conversations that are beneficial for the leader and for the team member. These sessions could be based on a documented plan, but while documentation is a nice summary for the leader and team member (and yes, even for legal and HR), the actual *conversation* is where the magic happens. I learned to ask three questions:

1 What are you most proud of in the last year? In the last six months?
2 Is there anything you would have done differently?
3 What do you need from me going forward?

The questions are simple, but there was some art to making this conversation successful. Prior to the meeting I would sit down and answer these questions myself with regard to the team member's contributions. During the actual conversation, I would pause after the first question and either add to team member's list of 'proud of,' or reiterate their comments in my own words. Likewise, I would add to the list of 'done differently,' or reiterate in my own words.

This was my best tool for constructive feedback, discovering what mattered the most to someone helped me understand their strengths and fulfillment. Pointing out accomplishments and contributions that a team member didn't necessarily see themselves was a way to open people up to their hidden strengths. Reflecting on what could have been done differently indicated whether or not learning took place, and if the constructive feedback from me and others resonated with the team member. Finally, having someone respond to 'what do you need from me?' sometimes uncovered a need I was not aware of, or simply reinforced where I could support them.

TAMMY

Actionable. Feedback should be actionable and clear, targeted to actions related to professional improvement. As with specificity, if feedback is not *actionable*, it simply does damage without a path forward. Direct, specific, and actionable feedback can be very effective in changing behavior, helping people grow and learn.

Hold individuals accountable

Holding individuals accountable does not come naturally for all leaders. Setting direction and planning, giving feedback and coaching, or removing roadblocks may be more natural talents for any leader. Holding individuals accountable for their job and their contribution to the team and the organization may come with some missteps at first.

Jeff Thompson, MD, author of *Lead True: Live Your Values, Build Your People, Inspire Your Community*, puts accountability in a unique light. He says, "Holding individuals accountable is looking backward. Being responsible for their success is looking forward. Superior performance will require a balance of the two."[13]

In today's business world, where 'data is king,' leaders have a number of resources *to look back at* to determine whether or not an individual is performing. We can pull reports, discuss them with our team members, resolve any conflicts, compliment their achievements, and call that 'accountability.' But achievement of goals is only part of high performance.

Thompson proposes that there is a large gap between doing and accomplishing. A player-coach needs to stay close enough to individuals' work to get beyond the numbers and understand a deeper effect of accomplishments. Leaders should ask individuals *how* they got to where they are, then actively listen. Maybe they *did* a lot but *accomplished* very little, in which case the leader needs to address whether the person is doing the right tasks.

The player-coach should also look at what it took to accomplish the work: do short-term wins set the team up for long-term problems? Are partner relationships being enhanced by how the work got done, or did partners get left in the dust? Are other performers in the department stronger, more energized, more engaged because of how work is being accomplished, or the reverse? The player-coach's role is to constantly help people succeed—including influencing the process by which people *get work done,* not just what gets accomplished.

The individual is accountable for their own outcomes, the player-coach is accountable for collective outcomes and for the growth and development of individuals and the team. Another way to think of this is that holding people accountable can seem like a 'ruling' task, when in fact it should be seen as a 'serving' task. A 'ruling' conversation may start like this: "Let's look at your numbers for the past week." A 'serving' conversation will go like this: "Let's think about your numbers for the past week. Was there anything that specifically influenced your results?"

As the player-coach discusses accountability with individual team members, they should be sure to incorporate the other techniques we've discussed so far, such as being direct and specific, so team members are crystal clear about expectations for what they should accomplish. A well-known goal-setting acronym is SMART: specific, measurable, actionable, realistic, and time-related. The leader should establish an expectation of achieving SMART goals and let individuals decide how they will accomplish those goals.

Having regular and consistent one-on-ones with team members and giving them honest feedback will help build a culture of accountability. The leader can then coach their team to be successful—supporting them with resources, contacts, or knowledge that will help them improve.

Stretch and motivate

Many leaders believe their role in team motivation is small and insignificant. After all, their team members are being paid to do their job, and it is their obligation to do it well. Good player-coaches know they have an opportunity to excite those they lead to manifest their discretionary effort, to go above and beyond going through the motions of their job. The player-coach's role is pivotal in aligning and motivating those they lead to do their best: starting by setting high standards and showing their team what they are capable of. When someone says that a player-coach had confidence in them when they didn't believe in themselves, it indicates that the player-coach understood how to motivate.

STRETCH TO DEVELOP

EARLY IN MY career, I was working for a large corporation that was dramatically affected by an economic downturn and a sea change in the demand for our products. Huge workforce cuts were planned, and I was brought into some of the meetings to determine how the announcements would be made, and what services and assistance we would provide the managers who were affected.

I missed a large portion of a planning meeting a few days before the announcement because of another commitment, and by the time I made it I had already been identified as the lead for efforts in providing assistance to those impacted. This meant providing job search workshops and career continuation assistance to hundreds of managers and, within a few months, thousands of hourly workers. We had never done anything like this before, and the magnitude of the effort was unparalleled in the company's history.

There was no time for a lot of research and best practices, or even much time to organize. Within days, we identified and built out some space in a vacant building for workshops, and for the impacted individuals to work on resumés, make phone calls, get counseling, and so on. Within a month, we replicated the space and workshop offerings in three different cities. 'We' (I) made so many mistakes in our efforts, yet it was an incredible development experience for me. I grew tremendously.

VAL

There is a lot of commentary in literature and in the news about generational differences and the changing makeup of the workforce. Over the years, with each generational shift, notions arise that those entering the workforce are driven by different values or perspectives than the current workforce. We create categories like Millennials, Gen Xers, Baby Boomers, etc., to describe workers who differ from their predecessors.

Today, there is a belief that Millennials—those who reached young adulthood in the early twenty-first century and are sometimes referred to as Gen Y or Gen Z—are driven by different values and want to be treated differently than Baby Boomers. In the macro sense, it may be true: there is research showing some differences between these generations, which is not surprising given the dramatic shift in environmental factors that has occurred in the last thirty or forty years. Search 'motivating Millennials' and you will find a myriad of tips on how to treat those who fall into this generational category.

The problem is, as we research suggestions on how to treat Millennials, we often find items that resonate with us as well (and we are Boomers!). That is, when we see suggestions on how to treat Millennials, most of the suggestions are how we would like to be treated. While on average there are sizeable differences between Millennials and, say, Boomers or Gen Xers, there also great differences *within* each of those groups. This is why good player-coaches understand that to motivate a particular person, they need to *know that person*, not the category they fall into. Some corporate policy decisions may be made based on changing demographics of the workforce, but the principle for a player-coach motivating their team is a constant: *know what drives the person individually and work with that to motivate for mutual benefit.*

In this sense, all motivation is local, just like the common phrase, "all politics are local." People are different from each other, and to shortcut the motivational process by assuming all people within a certain category have the same personal desires or attributes is a recipe for disaster.

For example, treating people as categories rather than as individuals can lead to unconscious bias on the part of the player-coach. One situation we are familiar with is when a high-performing employee became frustrated when her manager repeatedly overlooked her for critical assignments. This leader was the top performer in the group and all her peers were male. Several of these peers had been given responsibility for some critical assignments, and they were constantly coming to her for advice, perspective, ideas, and solutions.

Highly frustrated, she approached her manager over coffee one morning. "Why are you passing me over for critical assignments?" she asked, getting straight to the point.

"I didn't think you'd want the travel required for the assignments, given you are well into your pregnancy," he stammered.

"I wish you hadn't presumed what I want," she responded. What to him had seemed like a well-intended attempt to protect her had a very different impact on the high performer. Had he asked her if she wanted to be considered for such assignments, even expressing his concern, her reaction may have been very different.

It is equally ineffective for the player-coach to assume that what motivates them personally is also what motivates another. Again, all people are different, and what drives one may not drive another. All motivation is local. The wise player-coach will know what the members of their team want and will personalize their approach to ensure each member is motivated.

IF YOU EVER DO THAT AGAIN, I'M QUITTING!

I ONCE WORKED with a woman who was an excellent manager of logistics. She ran our conference center and was always on top of everything, and she curated an amazing experience for all who attended the activities held at the center.

She did such a good job that I wanted to reward her with a special bonus. To put a nice touch on it, I decided to present it to her in front of a large group who was participating in an event at the center. During the closing of their program, I took the mic, asked Pat to come forward, and presented her with the bonus to the applause of the crowd. She graciously accepted the award, but I sensed she was not comfortable or excited about what had happened.

After the program closed and the conference group departed, I had a chance to speak with her one on one before my departure. Her words still echo in my ears: "Val, if you ever do that again, I'm quitting! Don't you know I hate to get up in front of a crowd? Why would you make me do that?"

I tried the best I could to recover with something like, "I just wanted them all to know what you have done and for you to get the praise and recognition you deserve." However, those words were not helpful. To acknowledge and reward her most effectively, I had to do it in a way that most impacted her—not how I thought it should be, not so others could see, but how she wanted it to be.

We are all different. Pat wanted quiet recognition. Some want accolades and applause from others. Some want a little more money. And some just want the increased attention from the leader or to know they are contributing to a greater whole. To motivate someone, there is no substitute for knowing the individual.

VAL

If you are a member of a large organization, while you are reading this section you might be thinking that your incentive and compensation programs are one size fits all, and they have specific guidelines on how to distribute and present rewards. We understand that in a large organization, things typically have to be standardized. But the player-coach can make the 'standard' experience a little different for each person. Maybe some rewards are given privately, while others are presented in front of a group. Maybe the player-coach simply sends a note to the spouse or finds some funny way to highlight a moment. The special touch depends on what will be most appreciated by the individual. The leader should not just take the easy road and simply accept that there is a standard program and that they can't do anything unique or different.

It is also important to realize that motivation is not only based on rewarding compensation. Consistent with the perspective that we are all motivated by different drivers, not everyone is driven by dollars. While compensation is important—people should be paid what they're worth, and many people think money 'talks' in terms of telling them what their leader really thinks of them—the player-coach has many other tools they can use to motivate and inspire. Other actions that 'talk' include giving people opportunities to work on mission-critical assignments, present to upper management, or get training or educational opportunities. The list is almost endless, limited only by the player-coach's creativity. Again, not every opportunity will motivate everyone—all motivation is local. The leader must understand what motivates each individual.

So how does a player-coach get to know what drives those they lead? This comes more easily to some player-coaches than to others, and it doesn't always come by simply asking people what drives them. Some people will know exactly what motivates them and will seize the moment to share. But others may not be able to come up with the key to their motivation.

First, the player-coach should schedule a time to simply talk with each team member. Asking the individual where they would like to meet helps to confirm the meeting is about the team member and not the player-coach.

To help the team member prepare for the interaction, the player-coach should let them know what questions they want to ask and if there is anything they want to add to the agenda. We have found that the following questions can lead to a fruitful discussion:

- What is your end game? What do you want to do during your career? What do you want to achieve?

- What are your expectations of me? How can I assist you in your career? How can I best lead you?

- In the near term, how do you want to develop or grow? How can I assist in your development?

As the conversation unfolds, the player-coach should make notes rather than rely on memory: after all, "a dull pencil lead is more accurate than the sharpest mind." (Today that translates into "a poorly formatted Word doc without a spell check is better than a well-organized mind meld.")

After the conversation, the player-coach should continue to observe and learn. Is the team member acting consistently with what they said they wanted? By continuously staying informed about what drives the individual, the player-coach can help them be their best selves. The better they are, the better the team is.

It is also important for the player-coach to ensure that those they lead are not frustrated by roadblocks or a lack of resources, as we discussed in Chapter 3. The leader's best intentions will fall flat if they are not willing to remove roadblocks, provide support, and advocate for those they lead. This is something that only the leader can do and is critical to motivating the team to excel.

"Coaching isn't therapy. It's product development with you as the product."

FAST COMPANY[14]

5

BUILD
TEAM

"I HAD THREE truly great high-performing teams in my entire thirty-year career. It takes a long time to get them there, and you have to put the right people in place. Often leaders are not in place long enough to see it through. To get them there, I asked many, many questions, and after a while they were anticipating what I was going to ask—they had the answers! Things began moving faster. I moved faster too. I never wanted to be a roadblock; I wanted to remove roadblocks. If you want teamwork, you have to drive it and be a role model. You have to think of all members of the team."

FORMER CIO IN THE TELECOMMUNICATIONS INDUSTRY

Set Direction

Secure Resources

Build Team
- Communicate to inspire
- Leverage the team
- Motivate
- Recognize
- Build trust

Coach Individuals

IN THE PREVIOUS chapter, we discussed the approaches player-coaches can apply when coaching, developing, and motivating individuals on a team. We stressed that focusing on each team member's unique desires for development, recognition, and reward is at the heart of coaching individuals. Successfully leading a team begins with establishing leadership with each team member.

We strongly believe that when it comes to team-building, strategy is essential for all levels of leadership. There are many ways to approach team-building—some may even require huge investments of time, energy, and money—but before investing heavily in anything specific, the player-coach should make sure they have the right balance of talent on their team. If the player-coach wants to bring in, change, rotate, or even excuse any individuals, this should be done prior to investing in team-building. See the section on putting talent in the right places in Chapter 3 (page 47) for more on getting the right people in the right roles.

Once the player-coach has the right people in place, they still have to build the team: simply having the players does not make the group a team. Here are the five actions we have identified for the player-coach to consider when building an effective team.

Communicate to inspire

Communication is key in team-building. It is important for the player-coach to not only communicate directly, openly, and honestly *with* the team, but also foster good communication *among* the team members. The relationships between team members are as important as those between the team and the player-coach. The player-coach should encourage trust, cooperation, healthy communications, and respect within their team: think of this as establishing a communications culture for the team.

Establishing a team's unique mission, vision, values, and goals aids in creating an effective communications culture. While the player-coach will usually focus on defining these things when they are first placed in a role, or at the beginning of each evaluation year, they can be defined (and refreshed) at any time. By involving team members in this task (as discussed in the vision section of Chapter 2, page 35), the player-coach creates the opportunity for open and healthy communications with, and among, the team.

Communicating for alignment also involves the team's culture and work environment. Unless the player-coach is the CEO, the culture of the team will follow the tenets of the larger organizational culture. But any function, organization, or team within a larger organization has (or has the opportunity to have) a little uniqueness and culture of their own, and the player-coach is responsible for ensuring that this culture is positive and fitting for the function and organization. Good player-coaches make sure the conditions in which their team works are positive and that the team feels supported, purposeful, and challenged.

Ironically, it is often the player-coach who introduces dysfunction to a team, or a skewed alignment with the greater organization. This may not be intentional, and the player-coach may not even realize they are doing it. The player-coach may want to have an aligned and functional team, and may even participate in team-building sessions or visioning sessions where the right statements are made and the direction is identified. However, if the player-coach's actions depart from those desires, or are seen as departing from them, that player-coach introduces confusion and misalignment to the team. The phrase "a picture is worth a thousand words" has a parallel in business life: "A leader's actions say more about his or her values, direction, and desires than any mission statement or values list." The stated values may be on the wall, but the actions of the player-coach and the actions of the team that are rewarded and reinforced describe the real culture of the organization.

There will be disputes, arguments, disagreements—better yet, healthy points of debate—within any team. The player-coach is a harmonizing influence, and it is their job to resolve and mediate disputes, constantly directing the debate toward the team's goals, while being sensitive to any unspoken feelings or attitudes, and drawing those out in a positive way.

The player-coach needs to constantly encourage their team to communicate with each other, and this can be achieved by delegating problem-solving: a team who works together to find solutions will create their own form of healthy communication. The player-coach should also work with the team to encourage the practices of active listening (see Chapter 6, page 103), brainstorming, and building consensus. The last can take shape in different ways (e.g., voting, risk analysis), so the team should discuss and agree on how to reach consensus.

Leverage the team

Great player-coaches learn to leverage their teams strengths, and great companies understand that effective teams are the vehicles for accomplishing important work. While individuals can be great at their jobs and performing specific work, the blending and use of their skills as a team can lead to high performance. Getting a team to high performance is the work of the player-coach.

We know a player-coach who managed a group of data analysts and used an effective technique to leverage her team's skills. The team's primary work activities included:

- acquiring data from multiple sources;
- maintaining databases;
- interpreting data;
- developing and implementing data analyses;
- knowing and understanding data collection systems and other strategies that optimize statistical efficiency and quality;
- analyzing results; and
- using statistical techniques.

The player-coach evaluated her five team members on each of these skill areas using a simple points system: 1 = top performer; 2 = good performer; and 3 = performance below expectations. After reflecting on the overall skills of the team, the player-coach was able to use some team members to coach others in certain areas, invite other experts into staff meetings for a group learning exercise, and make specific courses available for other members of the team.

This exercise gave the player-coach a picture of what development was needed for the team as a whole, and for each individual. She was able to map an effective course for development and assess it again at a later date.

Motivate

We discussed motivating individuals in detail in Chapter 4, and now we will discuss why motivating a team is also important and the two aspects to consider—one uses a broad lens and one a narrow lens.

Let's first look at how player-coaches can focus with a broad lens: it is important to remind your team of their contribution to a greater organization, how their work has a bigger purpose. While annual company bonuses (those achieved by everyone in the organization for accomplishing a few key outcomes) are meaningful, reminding the team how they contribute to that achievement will give the monetary award a personal meaning.

Another way to motivate the team is to seize opportunities to try new things within a department or company (e.g., be the first group to move into a new space; volunteer to lead a company-wide effort), though the player-coach should always ask the team if they want to be first to the plate. Not only will opportunities like this foster teamwork, they will also elevate the team's profile company-wide.

Player-coaches should also reflect on more focused motivation: what is a specific motivator for the team? Take the work environment for example, everyone wants their workplace to be clean, stimulating, and simply 'make you feel good.' If there are tangible variables that are within the player-coach's control to change (keeping break rooms clean, recycling for the environment, sponsoring or participating in a local charity event), they should activate the group to bring about the changes everyone can agree on. If the desired changes are beyond the player-coach's decision-making capability (painting walls, installing new carpet, acquiring new office furniture), the player-coach should be a champion for those changes and keep the team informed on the status.

It is the leader's role to encourage a positive work environment, and often the first step is to define what specific attributes matter the most to their team—and then get creative with developing the kind of workplace everyone desires. For some teams it might mean 'everyday casual attire,' for others it might mean 'sports Fridays' (wear your favorite jersey and cheer for your sports team). Here is a list of other fun things to do at work:

- Decorate the workplace once a month. Pick a theme (e.g., February = love, June = beach, September = football) and go for it! Rotate the decorating 'privileges' among small groups.

- Have a sports tournament. Pick a day and have a putt-putt tournament at the office. Have each person (or small groups) design a putt-putt hole. You will be surprised—people can get very creative. Ask others in the workplace to participate by paying a dollar to play the entire course. Give the proceeds to charity, buy a few backpacks for schools, or fill a stocking for a needy child during the holidays. One team leader we know actually created an 'Office Olympics' with five or six events (wastepaper toss, paper clip field goals, etc.) and blocked off an afternoon so everyone could compete.

- Playing off of the movie *The Bucket List* with Morgan Freeman and Jack Nicholson, create a 'bucket list' bulletin board where teams can pin up bucket list items, or attach their name to existing items. You would be surprised how many team members have similar bucket list items (hang gliding, visiting all fifty states, visiting all MLB ballparks, etc.). This simple activity can connect team members in a totally different way.

Recognize

Player-coaches can best recognize the team by creating a culture of appreciation. Let's face it, it's a busy world out there and no one has the cure for insufficient time. However, showing teams or individuals they are appreciated isn't a matter of time and intention, but of priority and action. Creating a culture of appreciation starts with the player-coach, and then others will want to 'give appreciation away.'

Celebrating accomplishments (personal and professional) and genuinely showing pride in the team are great ways that a player-coach can show appreciation. Here are some other not-so-new, but sadly underused, actions to help instill appreciation:

- Say thank you and do thank-yous. Yes, say it out loud for all to hear, and decide at other times to write thank-yous (notice we said *write*, not *type*).

- Offer options when it comes to new projects for the team to work on and let them pick one as a group. This will solidify their buy-in to working on something they know is important.

- Let the team present their work to the boss.

- Take the team to lunch or bring in breakfast to say thank you.

- Leave a candy message on everyone's desk. ("You've been a lifesaver" = roll of Life Savers.)

Within a culture of appreciation, there are other things player-coaches can do to offer recognition to teams, such as host an after-action review when a big project is complete. The purpose of the review is not to pick apart what did or didn't happen, but for the team to share successes and spawn other ideas before tackling the next project. Hosting a review gives the player-coach the opportunity to communicate satisfaction with the outcome(s), to talk about how people grew in the process of working together, and to generate positive energy around what the team can accomplish next.

Another reward may be that of time: the player-coach can surprise their team with a half-day off that won't be counted against their vacation. This likely can't happen very often, but when it does, it will always be remembered. Think about the excitement when a team member surprises their family or friends by coming home early or having a half-day off with them. This reward has a positive effect not only on the team member, but also on those who support them outside the workplace.

Recognizing a team could also take shape in the form of helping others. If a team is passionate about its community or a cause, give them time to volunteer as a reward for their hard work and contributions. If done as a group, this is an excellent way of team-building. For example, some companies allow one full day of service per year per employee. If pursuing such an idea, the player-coach should let their team pick a project that would be most meaningful to them.

A player-coach who knows their team members' interests, drivers, and aspirations will be able to pick the perfect activity to motivate them. Allowing the team to suggest and plan the activity can generate even more of an investment.

Build trust

As leader, coach, advocate, and role model, a player-coach's first responsibility in any situation is to their team. When the team sees that their leader 'has their back,' they will have the leader's back as well.

There are several tenets to building this kind of trust. The player-coach must:

- Do what they say they will do. Their word is *golden* and everyone is watching: if something happens and the leader can't do what they said, they must be humble enough to go back to the team and let them know why.

- Have the courage to defend and face the team. The leader *is* the team when the team is not around. When peers or supervisors question the team's actions or output, the player-coach must stand up for, and own them. Likewise, if the team is upset or dismayed by larger issues within the department or organization, the player-coach must face them and help them through it.

- Avoid playing favorites. It's natural that some personalities will align more than others, but the team must trust the player-coach to guide and direct their work fairly. Playing favorites erodes that trust.

- Be very clear in communication. The player-coach should let their trust in the team be part of what's communicated and use the word 'trust' in what they say.

- Face conflict. Rather than avoid conflict, the player-coach must face it and keep their actions, thoughts, and words in check.

- Keep confidential *confidential*. If someone on the team asks for confidence, the player-coach should respect that and never betray it.

Effective player-coaches also build accountability inside the team, and self-accountable teams will:

- identify problems and opportunities early by questioning one another;

- make sure poor performers or people not carrying their weight feel and know they need to improve;

- move past or avoid bureaucracy; and

- quickly establish respect among team members who have high standards and therefore bring up the overall standards of the team.

> **"The way a team plays as a whole determines its success. You may have the greatest bunch of individual stars in the world, but if they don't play together, the club won't be worth a dime."**
>
> BABE RUTH[15]

PART

CRITICAL SKILLS

AND GROWTH

THREE

When we coach executives, we often give them a report outlining their strengths and development opportunities. Many have gone home to a spouse or significant other and shared the report, only to hear them say, "I hope you didn't pay much for that report. I have been telling you that for years."

6

CRITICAL SKILLS

"I LEARNED THE critical skills of leading from good training programs, and also from having good and bad supervisors. The training was additive, but it was the application of training that solidified my skills. I see supervisors today struggling to make the transition. It seems they are resistant to picking up the new people skills or soft skills needed to lead, and to relinquishing some of the detailed expertise. I am now 75 percent leading and 25 percent expert as an executive."

CHIEF PEOPLE OFFICER IN THE BUILDING
PRODUCTS INDUSTRY

Observe

Listen

Delegate

Communicate

Build effective
relationships

Organize and plan

Be a role model

THIS CHAPTER FOCUSES on the skills that are critical to succeed as a player-coaches. We will explore each of the significant skills that are essential to leading people *and* leading the function, and also offer suggestions for how to grow these skills. The tips are not meant to be definitive exercises; rather, they are suggestions upon which others can build and assist in player-coach development.

Everyone is capable of developing and refining these skills if they focus their efforts. Some of these skills will come easier to some player-coaches than to others, and some player-coaches will never master all of them. That's okay—we are all different! A player-coach doesn't have to be a master of *all* of these skills to be successful.

These skills are not presented in a specific order of importance. A player-coach should *use* their strengths, not *overuse* them. Just as we cautioned about the overall player-coach success model—that all four aspects are important, but that an individual player-coach won't focus on each aspect 25 percent of the time—we give a caution about skills. Each skill we discuss is important, but not all skills are equally important at any one time. A player-coach may be very good or become very good at one thing, but if that's the only skill they employ, it will become a liability.

What's the distinction between developing a skill and managing a skill? Sometimes a thoughtful and strategic player-coach may struggle with a particular skill, and they can manage this by ensuring the skill is well represented by those they lead, and then leaning on those players when required.

It is important for the player-coach to be aware of their weaker skills and to ensure that they are sufficiently developed to succeed on the job. A player-coach who cannot, or does not, want to grow one or more of these skills may want to reflect on whether they do in fact want to coach or, rather, only use their skills in a player role.

For player-coaches, now is a good time to pause and conduct a self-assessment on these skills. Ask yourself:

- What feedback—positive or constructive—have I received about any of these skills?
- Have I ever struggled to demonstrate any of these skills?
- Do any of these skills come more naturally to me than others?

In the spirit of engaging others in your growth and development, consider showing the graphic to your manager, your colleagues, or those you lead, and asking, "Where do you see me as strong in these areas, and where do you think I could grow?" You might also ask your spouse or significant other. We often give an executive feedback or an assessment report outlining their strengths and development opportunities, and when they share the report with their spouse or significant other, their response is, "I hope you didn't pay much for that report. I have been telling you that for years."

One more note about learning and developing these skills: it is a mistake for a player-coach to try to improve four or five skills at once. This will likely result in no more than incremental progress on any of them. It is more effective to put a laser-focus on developing one or two skills at a time. With an intentional focus for three to four months, the needle of improvement is likely to move significantly more than when efforts are spread across all the skill areas at once.

Observe

At first blush, the idea of 'observation' may seem out of date, since many of today's workers actually provide information or perform intellectual work that can't be physically observed. As well, many teams are virtual, so physical observation is simply not feasible.

But observing should not be thought of just as watching someone work: it also means to observe or review work output like products, reports, or comments by clients, coworkers, and partners. Observation doesn't have to be conducted on a daily basis, but it should be a regular activity, rather than something that is done after months or years of leading someone.

Here are some tips for how a player-coach should observe those they lead.

Give them wings. A player-coach can provide opportunities for their team members to present, discuss, lead, and facilitate, and then can observe how the team performs in those situations. This may not involve physically watching the person. For example, with a virtual team, the player-coach can ask someone to facilitate a virtual meeting and 'observe' how they do. If a team member presents to a client, the leader can observe this directly, or follow up with the client and ask for their views on how the person represented themselves.

Think of it this way: it is very hard to coach and motivate people to be the best they can be without seeing what they do, watching how they perform, and talking to those with whom they work.

Review their work. A critical aspect of observing is the task of reviewing others' work. This is especially relevant in the world of subject matter experts, where the work product may be a report, a presentation, a written thought piece, or some other material that the player-coach is very familiar with.

When reviewing work, the player-coach should keep three things in mind:

1. Monitor substance, not form. Don't worry about fonts and style, ensure the information is credible. Set expectations that the work product should be of the highest quality and have the greatest impact.

2. Embrace different approaches. When giving someone the responsibility to do something, the player-coach should accept that it doesn't have to be done the same way as they would do it. Suggest that the team member enlists the knowledge and input of peers for trial runs; this can help to ensure that feedback on content and approach is captured in advance.

3. Don't get too close. The player-coach is not responsible for proofing a report, for example—others can do that effectively and efficiently. Don't hover or get in the weeds. Allow the high performer to thrive and grow on their own while supporting them with encouragement. Don't reinforce poor performance by doing the work of the poor performer without addressing the performance issues directly. The player-coach's work is not to *correct the product,* but to help *change the performance* of the one who creates the product.

Practice feedforward instead of feedback.[16] The easiest way to understand the difference between conventional 'feedback' and 'feedforward' is to think in terms of the past and the future. Conventional feedback is past-focused: it provides information about past activity and performance. Feedforward, on the other hand, is future-focused: it provides information about what a person could do differently in the future. These suggestions for improvement enable people to make ongoing adjustments in how they are performing. Feedforward focuses on the variety of things that *can* be, not the limited things that *have* been. This difference has a profound effect on how the conversation might go, and therefore on the motivation and engagement of employees.

Another key reason to use feedforward rather than feedback is that feedback is typically delivered poorly. Many player-coaches tend to focus only on what's gone wrong. As a result, not only do many employees dislike receiving feedback, but many player-coaches dislike giving it, and may even avoid providing it when it really is needed.

Get multiple points of feedback and own it. When we speak to effective player-coaches, it is clear that feedback is gathered in different ways. Some carefully review the output of the individual, any reports produced, and any data that shows how effective and efficient they are. Often the effective player-coach has regularly scheduled one-on-ones with team members to see how things are going and to ask about any issues they are facing. Some player-coaches prescribe specific assignments so they can observe and gather information to assist the player. Some are very attuned to their colleagues' perspectives and comments about members of the player-coach's team. This doesn't mean that a comment by a colleague or a partner can make or break a player, but the wise player-coach merges such feedback with their own observations and other objective data.

There may be times when a player-coach is not proactive about observing their team and may rely heavily on what a colleague or another team member may say about an individual. While such input can be meaningful, it can also lead to conclusions that are way off base if taken without other data and inputs. A player-coach should make their own first-hand observations and form their own perspectives of each member of their team. To do that, the player-coach must establish a routine of observing and gathering information. This is an important skill and practice to strengthen as it becomes a natural part of leading, coaching, and motivating.

Understand behavior, don't judge behavior. Jumping to a conclusion about the intent of the person being observed can be dangerous and lead to poor decisions. When a player-coach sees a behavior, they should recognize it for what it is: *behavior*. The person's intent or thoughts can't be observed. To understand the intent or purpose behind the behavior and to come to an accurate conclusion, it is best to have a good discussion with the person—one that includes non-judgmental questions regarding their behavior. Such a conversation will also be helpful in coaching the individual, discussing the effectiveness of the approach, and identifying what may be more effective going forward.

Listen

Listening is a skill we can *all* work on. When we talk about 'improving our listening skills' it is not our *hearing* we are trying to improve (that may include some different technology), rather it is referring to our 'active attention' to what is being said. Are we actually listening to the extent that we can converse and add value to the full conversation, as opposed to the one that is happening in our heads? Here are some tips for becoming a better active listener.

Learn how to actively listen. Player-coaches must *learn* the art of active listening. Once mastered, the player-coach will build rapport with their team members, have a better understanding of what is going on, and nurture an environment of trust.

To actively listen, the player-coach must:

- fully concentrate (get rid of all distractions);
- understand (have a full grasp of the facts, opinions, and emotions);
- respond (address the person talking with confidence and care); and
- remember what is being said (have the ability to repeat back to that person or to another audience).

Put active listening into practice. Active listening is one skill where practice doesn't make *perfect* (it's a big stretch to be perfect at active listening), but the more a player-coach practices active listening, the better they will become. Here are tips for intentionally practicing active listening:

- Every now and then restate what the person said, paraphrasing in your own words. You can start with, "Let me repeat what I've heard you say so far..." Comments like, "If I understand you correctly, you are saying..." or "So I hear you saying..." are reassuring and show you have heard *and* understand.

- At the conclusion of listening, summarize for clarity. Bring the problem/opportunity, facts, and perspectives all together with a phrase like, "Let me see if I can summarize all I have learned about this situation."

* Probe if you don't have a full grasp of what the speaker is saying. This allows you to draw the speaker out and get more information. "What do you think the outcome would be if you . . ."

* Include reflection in your dialogue as you summarize and restate. Reflect the speaker's words in terms of feelings. "This seems highly important to you . . ."

Hold your tongue. Active listening means just that: listening, not talking. When a player-coach interrupts frequently, the speaker may conclude that the player-coach is not interested in what they are saying. The player-coach should also be careful not to patronize or preach to the speaker—the leader is there to listen, not to tell or to advise. There may come a time when the player-coach gives advice, but not during active listening. It's crucial to put some time between listening/understanding and giving advice for next steps. There are plenty of times when the player-coach can and should ask, "Why?" But they also must recognize that a 'why' question can seem defensive. The player-coach should learn to use open-ended questions like, "What options have you thought of?"

Stop and pay attention. The biggest barrier to active listening is multitasking. Some people are incredible multitaskers, but research shows that we are less effective at functioning while multitasking than some might think.

While the fact that we can walk and talk at the same time suggests we can multitask, our brain actually finds it difficult to concentrate on two things at once, especially if what we are focusing on is anything but ingrained routine. We are just not good at it.[17] The brain may be a heck of a processor and capable of doing two things in very rapid order—but when it does, it is very *rapidly* handling only one thing at a time. When we are rapidly processing multiple tasks, we are *not completely focused* on any one issue. In the context of a conversation or a meeting, this comes across as not being *completely* present.

We had a colleague we used to like to tease about his actions during group meetings. He was constantly multitasking on his computer, no matter the situation. Over time, all jokes, puns, and jabs aside, we came to expect it rather than point out the disrespect. However, when it was his turn to speak, suddenly the multitasking ceased, which caused others to believe he was arrogant and rude. It took years of leading others and having literally hundreds of people point out his excessive multitasking (arrogance and rudeness) before he put the computer away.

A player-coach must build their listening skills, and that starts by paying attention. When a team member enters the player-coach's office or space, the latter shouldn't say, "Go ahead, I'm listening," if they are still typing away on a computer. When a leader speaks with someone they lead, they should be present—not clearing an inbox, not susceptible to whatever message comes across their phone—but focused solely on the other person and their issue. If it's not possible to be fully present, the player-coach should indicate when they *can* connect.

Encourage the dialogue to continue. Some employees who may be a little more intimidated by their leaders, or who are shy and introverted, may need to be encouraged to talk. The player-coach may need to offer encouraging words and pointedly help the person communicate. They can nod their head as the team member speaks, reinforce their comments, or preface questions with an acknowledgment or encouragement to further the dialogue: "I heard you say [blank] and I like that. What ideas do you have for [blank]?" or "I think you may have some valuable ideas or input. Can you describe [blank]?" The more experience the player-coach and team member have with each other, the more direct the player-coach can be. With a reluctant speaker, the player-coach should close each interaction with a positive acknowledgment of the conversation and gratitude for the person's efforts.

Get to the point. Sometimes a speaker can be verbose and get lost in tangents as they relay information. The player-coach can encourage them to be more succinct by asking them to 'boil it down' to what they need or what they are trying to say.

A woman we once worked with was so verbose that people simply struggled to listen. She embodied the statement, "You asked what time it was, and she told you how the clock worked." This person—who by the way was excellent at what she did and was loved by many—always threw in a short lesson on the history of clock-making. We wanted to pay attention, but we invariably found ourselves looking for something else we could do while she was talking. Everyone finally became accustomed to (comfortable with) asking her to *boil it down*. We began using questions like: "What do I need to know and do? How can I help you?" When we helped her be concise, we were able to be more effective in supporting her.

We recently gathered feedback about an executive through a 360-degree feedback process, and one of the themes for development was related to listening skills. One direct report commented, "I just want her to listen, not to solve my problems." People often want to bounce ideas off their leader so that they, in turn, will have the confidence to act. If the leader steps in and does everything for them, it not only takes the wind out of their sails, but also reinforces their reliance on the player-coach to do something when it should be the individual player's role to do. Clearly, there will be times when something must fall back onto the player-coach's desk, but by far the biggest error made by player-coaches is to get into the game when their player(s) simply want a listening ear.

Delegate

Delegation is a fundamental skill that can differentiate a struggling player-coach from a successful player-coach. A player-coach might actually get by without developing the skill of delegation, but one more promotion or increase in the scope of their role will likely mean disaster either professionally, personally, or both. A player-coach must learn how to distribute work to others and let them do the work.

Many think delegating simply means 'giving work to others.' But it is more than just keeping one's own desk clean. Here are some steps to effective delegation.

Set clear expectations. When delegating, it is critical to set expectations regarding the work that is being delegated: think in terms of delegating responsibilities, not tasks. This means providing a good explanation and context for the project or function being delegated, and likely spending more time with players up front to ensure they understand the responsibility and have the opportunity to ask questions before they begin. The player-coach should be clear on what respective roles will be, and address timelines, deadlines, and milestones. If there are others who are critical to the success of a given project or function, the player-coach should introduce them to the person being delegated to.

Agree on communications. The player-coach must ensure the person to whom they are delegating understands the expectations for communications. How often does the player-coach want to hear from them? Does the player-coach prefer to have a regular cadence of meetings or to communicate on an as-needed basis? Who is going to communicate to external constituencies and how will that happen? Does the player-coach want to be copied each time, or only by exception? Alignment on these kinds of communications is important when delegating. Without this alignment, it is easy to conclude, sometimes erroneously, that the delegation relationship is working, and the player-coach might be right back in the fray of whatever it is they delegated.

LEARNING TO DELEGATE

DELEGATING CERTAIN THINGS to a team member is a learned behavior. It was especially difficult for me early in my career, because there were, quite frankly, things I loved to do that took my mind off everything else. I'm not quite sure exactly where I picked up a delegation technique that worked for me, I can only remember that it was during the first ten years of my career (the player-coach years), and I hung on to it from then on.

I've always been organized and referred to as a 'planner,' so when it came to delegation I simply made a list of what needed to be done and presented it to my team in a staff meeting or some other planning opportunity. While the goals and objectives were clear, the list of what needed to be accomplished was up for grabs: meaning the team could modify it based on everyone's input. I simply provided the starting point. Then as a leader, I asked who wanted to do what. In some instances ownership was logical, and in others it meant there was an opportunity for people to volunteer for things out of their comfort zone, or for things they had an interest in but were not part of their normal job.

It wasn't at all scientific, and over the years I accepted that I wasn't great at delegation. I knew that my best contributions were in setting clear goals and objectives and facilitating a team process to figure out the 'what and how' of getting things done.

TAMMY

Stay out of the way. This may be one of the most difficult things to do, especially for player-coaches who are perfectionists and have team members with different approaches to the role or who want to try new things.

When delegating, the player-coach must not smother or hover: it is best to communicate the expected results and let the team member determine the way they meet the expectations. Trust is a big part of delegating, and the player-coach can build it by starting with smaller-scoped responsibilities. As trust grows and those being delegated to gain confidence, the player-coach can provide more opportunity and larger scope.

We often hear from colleagues who claim they can't get the work done the way they want it by delegation. That can't be a way out of delegating—it is the player-coach's job to ensure they have team members who they can delegate to. When we hear that complaint, it either means the player-coach is too picky (regarding people or work) and can't let go, or they are not playing the leadership role to ensure they have the right talent in place. A player-coach must ensure they have the right folks in place and allow team members to use their strengths to get the work done. The player-coach must stay out of the way.

Remove roadblocks. When issues arise that are beyond the 'pay grade' or capability of those who have been delegated the work, the player-coach's role is to remove the roadblocks so the work can move forward. The player-coach may have to defend and advocate for what the team member is trying to do. Some examples of common roadblocks are insufficient equipment or budget, an executive who doesn't respond to a meeting request, or a lack of alignment with a partner who needs to collaborate. One strategic phone call or an intentional connection between the player-coach and a colleague can move the work forward.

Sometimes removing roadblocks will take some courage and effort on the player-coach's part, and these may not be the most comfortable conversations or interactions. Nonetheless, a player-coach's effectiveness may depend heavily on their willingness to stand up and push forward. A leader who is willing to cover their team's back, stand up for them, and fight for what the team feels is important will solidify their position as a leader. Even if the player-coach is not successful in removing the roadblock, the team will respect them for putting forth a solid effort on behalf of their work. Removing roadblocks is an essential part of delegating: it may not happen often, but when it is needed, it is highly valuable.

Acknowledge effort and give credit. Part of delegating is recognizing what the delegate is doing and acknowledging that, individually and collectively. When someone shines, the player-coach should let them know it. When the time for accolades rolls around, the leader should make sure to give credit where credit is due and share any kudos received from others within the organization.

We have worked with executives and leaders who just can't seem to recognize and reward those they lead. Their reasoning is often, "I don't think it is right to recognize someone for doing the work I am paying them to do. If they do something exceptional or beyond expectations, I will recognize them, but not for doing their job." Our first thoughts when a client tells us that is, "Glad I am not their kid!"

While we are not suggesting that the effective player-coach give awards and recognition for doing adequate work, a leader can always acknowledge effort and a job well done. In the workplace, there is rarely *too much* acknowledgment and recognition (great emphasis on *acknowledgment*). The more a player-coach can show true pride in their team and acknowledge what they are able to accomplish, the more the player-coach will see the team accomplish!

Communicate

It seems obvious that a player-coach must be able to communicate to lead, and there are plenty of books about communication skills, but we want to break down the skill of leadership communication. We suspect it is more than what might initially come to mind.

Communicating as a player-coach takes on various forms: presentations to groups or teams, one-on-one communications, spontaneous comments and reactions in both group and one-on-one settings, messaging to the organization either orally or in writing, and even body language. Being an effective player-coach doesn't mean being a master presenter or an inspiring speaker. In fact, some of the most effective and inspiring speakers we have heard fail miserably in their leadership communications. But a player-coach must be a highly effective communicator to be the best leader they can be.

There are two main components in effective communications: the content of the message (what you say) and the delivery of the message (how you say it).

Content. The content of what we say is critical, but often in the hustle and bustle of our day-to-day world, we don't give enough thought to organizing the content of our message to ensure it is concise, compelling, and easily understood. Some might say, "It is just *my* team and I don't have to spend time preparing a speech every time I need to address *my* team." We are not talking about a full-blown TED Talk kind of preparation here. We are saying that the player-coach should take a few minutes to organize their thoughts most effectively before communicating a message to their team.

In Boyd Clark and Ron Crossland's *The Leader's Voice: How Your Communication Can Inspire Action and Get Results!*, they propose that most business communication is essentially incomplete. They write, "To make a memorable impression that will move people to act, communication must include three things: *data, emotion, and symbolism.*"[18] Most business communication includes data—and lots of it—but it really lacks any emotional or symbolic content. Here again, a brief message to one's team does not have to be an 'I have a dream' speech, but the more a player-coach can effectively organize the data or information they have to convey, attach it to an emotion or touch an emotion with it, and connect a symbol with it for memory, the more effective their communications will be.

We mention touching an emotion, and we know many business-minded professionals will balk at getting into the soft space in their communications. We aren't proposing a full-blown emotional plea: think of it more as connecting the message to a purpose or an event in someone's life.

THE CLOSEST PIECE OF PAPER SETS THE STORY

COMMUNICATION HAS ALWAYS been a passion of mine—I jokingly told my husband to inscribe my tombstone with "Say what you mean and mean what you say." I've worked hard over the years in leading teams (formal and informal) to strive for great (not perfect) communication. While some tools and techniques in various situations worked better than others, one technique by far wins the race.

Whenever I'm preparing to speak to an audience, or even composing an important document or email that will go to a team, I write things out long-hand. That's right! I do not start with the closest keyboard—I use the closest writing instrument and any piece of paper and jot out my first thoughts. It's my way of developing themes, finding the best words for the situation, and organizing or constructing the order of my thoughts. Once my stream of consciousness is out on paper, I then develop a basic outline (nearest Mac device in hand).

Everyone has to find their best, most effective communication patterns, tools, techniques, and styles. I'm a visual learner, so that initial piece of paper remains visually implanted in my head. Then, when I'm speaking, that piece of paper serves as a tool for me to visualize and remember the most important messages and context for an effective delivery.

TAMMY

You have probably heard the adage "tell them what you are going to tell them, tell them, then tell them what you told them" as an effective way to think about presenting. While we agree with this as a general organizing approach (demonstrated on the TED stage daily), be careful not to interpret this as 'repeat everything three times.' A better interpretation would be, "set the stage with a statement on the topic and the premise of what you are going to tell them; tell them the details, why they are important, and what the next steps are; then leave them with a statement that summarizes what we just discussed." The framework for organizing becomes: *set the stage, deliver the message, and close with a concise powerful statement that can be remembered and repeated.*

It is important that the team understands *why* they are being asked to do something. As leaders, when we give directions or instructions without giving context or purpose it can lead to decisions or actions that may even be contradictory to the overall objectives—simply because our team members are trying to follow the instructions *literally.*

Communicating the 'why' is essential to avoiding a broader, non-productive reaction in many situations. Consider these examples:

- A force reduction is necessary in a company, department, or organization. This may be the result of planned technology advancements in customer (self-)service and less calls to customer service departments. While these advancements will prove valuable to the customers and the company, the people affected must understand in advance that force changes are part of the improvement of the company.

- An annual team bonus payout was less than 100 percent. Why? While business may be good, the cost of raw materials was unpredictably at an all-time high this year, so expenses for the company exceeded the budget; and revenues did not exceed expectations to a degree necessary to make up the overrun in expenses.

And then there are the *everyday* situations when explaining the 'why' is helpful:

- Asking an employee to rerun a report. Why? Because upon reflection and interpretation of the first report, the player-coach wants to increase the time period for data collection to see if other patterns and trends appear or repeat themselves.

- Asking a peer coach to manage the team while a player-coach is out for a week of training. Why? Because the workload in the team is unusually heavy this time of the year and the player-coach wants all the team members to focus on their work rather than to ask one of them to be responsible for their work and the other leadership responsibilities.

When a team knows the 'why'—that is, the overall objective and why that objective is important—they can follow direction and adjust to ensure objectives are met rather than act in error or not fully comply with the organization's intent.

Delivery. Delivery of communication is as important as the content. A player-coach can gain or lose followers based on how they deliver their communications.

There are many books and other written materials available about communications and the delivery of communications, and we encourage player-coaches to seek out additional information, starting with *The Leader's Voice: How Your Communication Can Inspire Action and Get Results,* by Boyd Clark and Ron Crossland; and *Crucial Conversations: Tools for Talking When Stakes Are High,* by Kerry Patterson, Joseph

Grenny, Ron McMillan, and Al Switzler. For the player-coach, here are a few points we'd like to highlight about delivery.

First, the communicator should be mindful of what they are going to say, and they should spend a few minutes thinking through and even practicing their speech. We have been amazed at how confidence increases when player-coaches practice a speech or communiqué out loud rather than just thinking it through. One or two practice sessions makes a huge difference.

A few years ago, we attended an intensive speaking program with a half dozen close colleagues. Over the two-day course, everyone gave four or five brief speeches, or four or five portions of a longer speech. We found ourselves in a group with six raving extroverts who were not only willing to get up and speak, but who also fought to see who would go first—meanwhile, we hoped that the time would run out before our turns! Several of the attendees were professional speakers whose speaking engagements made up a significant portion of their revenue. These were close colleagues, but in the first hours of the class, we found ourselves not really wanting to be there. We had to remind ourselves that we were there for professional development, and that development is about *not always feeling comfortable.* We found the course extremely helpful, but probably most helpful was the notion that just a little practice and consciously thinking about style, movement, and delivery can pay huge dividends.

One of the best examples of effective delivery is the clarity in the following reprinted email allegedly penned by Elon Musk and sent to his entire organization. We highlight this email for its conversational clarity *and* its intent to establish a communications culture.

SUBJECT: COMMUNICATION WITHIN TESLA[19]

There are two schools of thought about how information should flow within companies. By far the most common way is chain of command, which means that you always flow communication through your manager. The problem with this approach is that, while it serves to enhance the power of the manager, it fails to serve the company.

Instead of a problem getting solved quickly, where a person in one dept talks to a person in another dept and makes the right thing happen, people are forced to talk to their manager who talks to their manager who talks to the manager in the other dept who talks to someone on his team. Then the info has to flow back the other way again. This is incredibly dumb. Any manager who allows this to happen, let alone encourages it, will soon find themselves working at another company. No kidding.

Anyone at Tesla can and should email/talk to anyone else according to what they think is the fastest way to solve a problem for the benefit of the whole company. You can talk to your manager's manager without his permission, you can talk directly to a VP in another dept, you can talk to me, you can talk to anyone without anyone else's permission. Moreover, you should consider yourself obligated to do so until the right thing happens. The point here is not random chitchat, but rather ensuring that we execute ultra-fast and well. We obviously cannot compete with the big car companies in size, so we must do so with intelligence and agility.

One final point is that managers should work hard to ensure that they are not creating silos within the company that create an us vs. them mentality or impede communication in any way.

This is unfortunately a natural tendency and needs to be actively fought. How can it possibly help Tesla for depts to erect barriers between themselves or see their success as relative within the company instead of collective? We are all in the same boat. Always view yourself as working for the good of the company and never your dept.

Thanks,
ELON

This email describes what most high-performing managers believe: that communication must flow freely in order to make quick and effective decisions. Notice how the email was sent directly to all employees and without a title or formal signature to close—simply *Elon*. Consistent with the powerful message sent in the body of the email, the informal first-name signature reinforces the informal and transparent culture this leader promotes throughout the organization.

Whether a team is 37,000+ as in Tesla, or just a few people, do they know the leader's perspective and expectations on information flow and communications? The wise player-coach will give some thought to their 'rules of communication' and the message they want to be heard.

One final thought: a leader's reaction to bad news, or to honest yet difficult information, is a major factor in setting the communication tone for the team. If a leader does not distinguish the messenger from the message, if they react in such a way that the messenger regrets ever bringing up the subject, the leader will conveniently close the channel to ever receiving such information—and that can be disastrous for both the leader and for the effectiveness of the organization. The player-coach may not like the bad news or difficult feedback, but how they react to it will signal much about their leadership and about their expectations for clear and transparent communications within the organization. We encourage leaders to communicate their expectations for honest communication throughout the organization, and to walk that talk when they get information that meets those expectations, even though it may not be what they would like to hear.

Delivering bad news is inescapable for a player-coach: it is not an easy or comfortable thing to do, but when a player-coach needs to deliver an uncomfortable message, it is critical that they do so in a way that the message is understood. Often the temptation is to soft-sell bad news, but this can prevent a clear message from getting through, which really does a disservice to those who ultimately need to hear it.

DID YOU HEAR WHAT I HEARD?

I HAD A great experience while I was participating in an executive development class that taught me the importance of being direct when delivering difficult news.

The leader of the session requested that half of the thirty-person class step outside of the room while he gave the remaining participants instructions on the role we were to play:

Your subordinate (those who left the room) has been working on a project for a while. They have been very engaged and excited about the project, and you, as manager have been supportive. This was not the only project they were working on, but it was clearly the favorite and most gratifying.

Unfortunately, you've just been told by your manager that the budgeting has been pulled and there is to be no further activity on the project. The company has decided to go in a different direction and the project will be shelved. We will have other work for those involved in the project, but they will be on hold for the time being. You are simply to tell your subordinate that the project is terminated and he or she should spend no more time working on it.

Those who left the room received the same information shared in the first paragraph, but they weren't told anything about the project being canceled. The subordinates were then invited back into the room, and we were all told to have a ten-minute conversation. Those of us playing the manager role all wanted to deliver the required message, but we wanted to do it in a way that did not demotivate our subordinates. We were all interested in ensuring that our employees were motivated and engaged.

I had what I thought was a good conversation with my 'subordinate,' kept him buoyed up, and showed concern for his feelings. Others similarly thought they had had good conversations and that the message was delivered.

When we reconvened as a total group to debrief the experience, the workshop leader asked, "Subordinates, how many of you are going to stop the project and put absolutely no more effort into it?" One hand went up. Of the fifteen subordinates, only one had actually heard the complete message that was to be delivered. The other fourteen had heard versions of the message that, wanting not to disappoint or demotivate, their managers had softened to the point that the subordinates felt they could continue to sell the idea, work on it in their spare time, or simply continue on as 'negotiations' regarding the future of the program continued.

I would like to say that my guy was the one who got the message, but he was not! That experience was decades ago, but the lesson still feels fresh to me.

VAL

Build effective relationships

Building effective working relationships is critical to success within organizations. It has always fascinated us, in our work with people in different organizations, that individuals will regularly say something like, "This place is unique in that here, you get things done through relationships." We say this is fascinating because, while there are differences between organizations, we have not seen an organization yet where relationships are NOT critical to getting work done. Organizations are different from each other in many ways, but the need for effective relationships in getting things done is almost universal in the world of work.

Part of the reason why a player actually becomes a player-coach is often because of their ability to relate and connect to people. However, that is not always the case. Nonetheless, to be successful, a player-coach must build effective relationships with their team and with peers, partners, and leaders. When we use the term 'effective relationship,' we mean a relationship where people trust each other and want to work together to get something done.

Here are some tips for building effective relationships.

Build trust. First let's consider how we build trust with others. We have all worked with colleagues who make a commitment but, more often than not, fail to keep that commitment. Our trust in these colleagues is not strong, so the first rule in building a trusting relationship is to be a partner who keeps your commitments.

To *keep* a commitment, you must first realize when you have *made* a commitment. A player-coach must be mindful when they have committed something to their team or others, and always keep that commitment—or have a very good reason why they cannot.

At times, we may do something, like nod passively to an idea or a request, without really realizing that this is coming across as a commitment. We can also do the opposite, suggesting we are more supportive of something than we really are. We know a colleague who received a good-natured roasting from his team at his retirement party. A team member got up and mentioned that their boss wasn't always direct when he communicated—you had to do some interpreting of the message he was sending. This person said that after several years of working for the retiring leader, he learned how to decipher much of what the leader said, and he presented some of these 'boss-isms' to the group. "When you presented a new idea to Hal and he didn't seem to be excited about it, he would say, 'That's an interesting idea. Let me think about it,'" this team member said. "When I heard that, I came to realize that the true message was, 'There is no way in hell this idea is seeing the light of day.'"

While this was relayed in good fun, we were struck by the idea that it should not take years of working closely together for our teams to understand what we are saying. Leaders should be explicit and direct in their communications if they want to build people's trust.

A player-coach has to be cognizant of what they are saying, and close enough to their team to be sensitive to what they are committing to or not committing to. Often the player-coach's commitments are focused on the client (internal or external) and to meeting whatever targets are set. If the player-coach can't meet those commitments, they usually communicate to the client to ensure they understand and can adjust their expectations. But sometimes player-coaches don't have the same level of commitment to those they lead—perhaps they expect team members to understand if things don't work out. We should have the same level of commitment to those we lead as we do to anyone who is expecting us to deliver, otherwise we cannot expect the full trust from those we lead.

Adopt an attitude of partnership. Building trust is a crucial aspect of building effective relationships—but it is not sufficient. Our colleagues may trust us completely, but if we are a pain to work with, or if we don't make it easy for them to connect with us, it is difficult to really have an effective working relationship.

What makes some people a 'pain' or affects others' willingness to work with them? In our years of coaching and working in and with organizations, we found that a couple of characteristics stand out.

The first is what we will term being 'rigid and right.' This is the person who is tough to work with because they always seem to act is if they have *the* answer and it is always *their* answer, and they will quickly point out the flaws in any other answer. Whether they are the smartest person in the room or not, they will act the part. Sometimes these people see everything as a point of principle, and any concession a compromise to that principle—but we must understand that the *principle of compromise* is different than *compromising one's principle*. In any organization there are going to be many views, and it is critical for us to consider them and work with others to find the best path forward, whether that is our idea or one coming from someone else. To be effective, the player-coach must be comfortable with considering others' ideas and approaches.

Another characteristic that negatively impacts a relationship is being 'bothered' by a request or interaction. We have probably all dealt with someone who makes it clear that they don't have the time or space for our request, no matter how small it is. These partners are usually very open with how busy they are and how crazy the pace is. But nobody has cornered the market on busy and crazy. The more one signals that they are too busy for colleagues, team members, etc., the more they wall themselves off from others. It may protect them from getting more work on their plate, but it is not likely to help them build healthy relationships and expand their impact.

A third characteristic that makes someone difficult to work with is being what we call a 'Debbie Downer': they see everything in the negative, worry about anything new or different, pick apart any idea, and give multiple reasons for why it will fail or be rejected. These folks may be very capable in their individual efforts, but they are not strong collaborators or connectors. Their negative energy usually outweighs the positivity their competency could bring to a relationship.

If these are some of the things that make people a 'pain' to work with, what characteristics and behaviors make someone a good working partner?

First is acknowledging and showing interest in others—their work, and their concerns—and taking time to listen, paying total attention. We can't tell you how often we hear commentary about how strong partners and collaborators "make me feel like I am the only one in on their mind, and I have their full attention." This is a great contributor to a relationship and especially important for a leader to show to those they lead, as it is easy to take them for granted and not pay them the attention they deserve.

Positivity is another great contributor to a relationship: most of us respond better to optimism than pessimism. This doesn't mean a rose-colored glasses naivete, but an optimistic 'we can get it done' attitude is a healthy addition to a partnership or collaboration.

Another behavior conducive to building relationships is reciprocity: asking the other person what you can do for them or looking for what you can do for them. Conventional wisdom says when you do something for someone, it is noticed, and it draws them closer to you. Looking for what you might do for someone is an effective way to build a relationship with them. A less conventional approach to building a relationship is found in some interesting research by Dr. Francis Flynn[20] and others at Stanford University. Their research found that while the receivers of assistance initially felt gratitude and positivity about the giver of assistance, that tended to wane over time, but the giver of assistance seemed to increase their positive feelings about their assistance over time.

WHAT DOES THIS all mean? Well, if you want to build a relationship then asking a favor of the other person will actually help you build that relationship. There is a great example of this principle in the autobiography of Benjamin Franklin.[21] In his autobiography, Franklin mentions a man who vehemently opposed his candidacy for Clerk of the General Assembly of the Pennsylvania House. No matter how much 'servile respect' (or kindness in today's terms) that Franklin showed, this individual's opinions on Franklin could not be changed. Interestingly, Franklin tried the exact opposite method, and it worked:

> Having heard that he had in his library a certain very scarce and curious book, I wrote a note to him expressing my desire of perusing that book and requesting he would do me the favor of lending it to me for a few days. He sent it immediately—and I returned it in about a week with another note expressing strongly my sense of the favor. When we next met in the House, he spoke to me (which he had never done before), and with great civility. And he ever afterward manifested a readiness to serve me on all occasions, so that we became great friends, and our friendship continued to his death.

This is another instance of the truth of Franklin's maxim that states, "He that has once done you a kindness will be more ready to do you another, than he whom you yourself have obliged."

Notwithstanding the wisdom of Benjamin Franklin, we can also use a bank account and the concept of making deposits before making withdrawals, as an analogy for building a relationship. That is, make sure you are doing as much or more for your partner than you expect from them.

Just as relationships with teams and colleagues are important, the player-coach must also build a trusting relationship with their own manager. Doing this is less about time spent with their boss and more about always being able to accurately provide the information they need, or accomplishing the task or goal given. Just as with colleagues, looking for ways one can help one's boss—and then following through—will strengthen the relationship. We often think of our relationship with our manager as being important for us, and it certainly is, but it is also important for our ability to represent and advocate for our team.

Organize and Plan

Player-coaches not only plan and manage their own time, but they also plan and organize their team's efforts. As soon as a player assumes leadership duties and becomes a player-coach, their perspective must extend further into the future to plan a path for those they lead.

We aren't going to go into full detail on organizing and planning here, but we want to provide a few insights from our experience of leading and watching leaders over decades. Here are some actions for player-coaches to consider when growing their organization and planning skills.

Make a system and a framework for all team responsibilities. The player-coach must prioritize and consider both the *important* work/task/products, as well as how the team will handle anything *urgent* when it arrives. While this will be a constant challenge, the objective should be to work mostly on the *important*, whether it is urgent or not, and to push anything of less importance to the back burner. This applies to the leader's own time as well as the efforts of the group.

- Take a basic inventory of the work the team is doing today. What is each person working on? What is the scope and/or timeline for each piece of work? Once this information is gathered, look at it as an entire body of work. Are some team members handling much more than others? Is the work generally allocated so that skills are matched to the work required? Is any of the work helping the person doing it to grow?

• Create a two-by-two matrix, with the importance of the work (high and low) on one axis, and urgency (high and low) on the other. Is the team doing any work that should be stopped or done differently?

High Importance Low Urgency	High Importance High Urgency
Low Importance Low Urgency	Low Importance High Urgency

Establish a structure and cadence for the team. Another aspect of organizing and planning is to establish a structure and cadence for the team. How often does the team meet as a group? Who establishes the agenda? How can the player-coach make the meetings meaningful and productive? How does the leader establish one-on-one touch points with team members? How does the player-coach manage their personal calendar *and* that of the team?

The player-coach's efforts here, or lack thereof, will have tremendous impact on the team. There is no single answer to how often or how much to meet, and there are lots of variations to the theme (from day-long staff meetings to frequent fifteen-minute standing huddles). The 'right' answer will depend on several factors, including the function and maturity of the team.

The key is to have a structure and cadence that the team can depend on and work to.

There are lots of ways to organize and plan, and a player-coach must find their own approach over time. For those who are not personally organized, we recommend reading *Getting Things Done* by David Allen, and *The First 90 Days* by Michael Watkins.[22] Implementing one or two (or more) practices or approaches out of these books will help a player-coach improve their personal organization.

Be a role model

We can all think about the list of bosses we've had and put them into two categories: those who we enjoyed working for and with, and those who we did not. Think about the teachers and the coaches you've enjoyed being around as opposed to those who didn't make it such a pleasant experience. The people who 'lead' us in life and work help to define role model behavior—either behaviors we want to emulate or behaviors we want to avoid. Positive role models make us want to be better people, better employees, and better leaders.

A player-coach should consider the role model qualities they hope others will use when describing who they are as a leader. While there is no specific formula for role models, as some careers and skill groups help shape a good role model, there are some common characteristics that most people look for in player-coaches.

Walk the talk. Employees want their leaders to do what they say they are going to do. 'Walk the talk' may be an overused statement, but it is also apt. If a leader communicates the importance of treating proprietary information as proprietary, yet puts proprietary documents in the general trash can, they cannot hold their team accountable for how they treat proprietary information. This is truly the essence of modeling. The player-coach must model what they tell others to do. Without that behavior, Ralph Waldo Emerson's adage rings true: "Your actions scream so loudly in my ears that I cannot hear what you are saying."

Be positive and confident. A good role model demonstrates confidence and is always positive, calm, and confident in who they are. This can be tough, but the leader sets the mood for the team. Related to staying positive and confident are other characteristics of being a good role model, like showing respect and concern for others, being humble, and being willing to admit mistakes. These moment-by-moment traits build confidence from within while outwardly treating others as they desire to be treated.

Openly communicate to all. People want bosses who use positive communication skills (active listening) and who communicate with everyone. Have you ever encountered a leader or teacher who addressed only a certain group of people most of the time? Those who were left in the cold likely performed their job (or participated in class) with less confidence and a weaker attitude.

Be a lifelong learner. Player-coaches who want to be great role models should focus on not only teaching others but being lifelong learners themselves. Being knowledgeable and well-rounded is a key trait of effective role models. People like to see leaders challenging themselves, learning, growing, and therefore building up the team.

Give back. Another key characteristic of great role models is that they think outside of the job and even outside of the company. These leaders care about giving back and cultivating that desire in those they lead. This could mean adopting or following a cause and working together as a team to support that cause. Some leaders find ways to pay it forward that support their career focus, like mentoring young professionals or students outside their company. Leaders who focus on good causes tend to have a strong commitment to their businesses.

"Words are singularly the most powerful force available to humanity. We can choose to use this force constructively with words of encouragement, or destructively using words of despair. Words have energy and power with the ability to help, to heal, to hinder, to hurt, to harm, to humiliate and to humble."

YEHUDA BERG, AUTHOR, SPEAKER, TEACHER, AND CO-DIRECTOR OF KABBALAH CENTRE INTERNATIONAL[23]

7

DEVELOPING PLAYER-COACHES

"I FOUND AS I rose in the organization I knew less and less of the specifics of the actual work we were doing. The actual terms of describing the work may change, but I found the concepts don't. So, to help player-coaches be more effective, I still lean on giving them expectations and demanding deliverables. But now their deliverables were focused on managing and leading and therefore different from when they were doing the work themselves. Their deliverables now may include a plan for the development of the team or a budget and timeline for a project. It's a different kind of output—one built on knowledge and intellect."

CHIEF TECHNOLOGY OFFICER IN
A COMMUNICATIONS COMPANY

I N THIS CHAPTER, we will discuss three topics. First, we'll describe the different ways a player might enter a player-coach role and offer some strategic advice. Next, we'll provide advice and insight for the player-coach who continues to be promoted and is now the coach of other player-coaches. Finally, we will provide information and guidance to those who are supporting player-coaches: human resources professionals, mentors, coaches, and so on.

Making the transition from player to player-coach

The transition from player to player-coach can take place in several scenarios:

- One player in a group of existing subject matter experts is asked to lead the group, so a peer of the group is promoted.

- An external recruit is placed in the player-coach role to lead an existing group.

- A player is performing a role, and with the expansion of the organization, the need to hire more talent into the function presents the opportunity for the player to build a team and become a player-coach.

All three scenarios involve the role of a player-coach as we have discussed throughout the book, and the information we have provided applies to each. However, we have some more specific advice to guide the player moving into the player-coach role in each scenario.

From peer to player-coach. Let's start with the player who starts coaching their peers. In this scenario, the player-coach knows the group, and the group knows the player-coach. This can often present a bit of a challenge. While ideally the team understands why the specific player was chosen to lead, invariably someone else in the group believes *they* should have been chosen or considered. Further, everyone is used to seeing the chosen leader as a peer, and it is a transition for everyone to now see the chosen player as the leader.

Michael Watkins' *The First 90 Days* (which we mentioned on page 129) provides excellent advice about shifting into a new role. We've also worked with hundreds of leaders in transition and here are a few specific tips from our experience.

It's important for the new player-coach to connect with each individual on the team individually and personally (face-to-face whenever possible); humbly express their excitement about working with the team; gauge the team's reaction and excitement; and enlist their support and engagement to make the team the best it can be. It's crucial that the player-coach listen to and read the team's reactions, desires, and interests.

This one-on-one connection is especially important to establish with anyone on the team who may have wanted the player-coach role themselves. Ideally this person will still be enlisted and engaged, however the player-coach will have to gauge the situation carefully. If it seems that will not be the case, the player-coach has to clearly and firmly communicate to the team member that their support is expected, or even offer to help them move to another role inside or outside the company. This can be a very difficult conversation, but it can also be a very rewarding one that will help cement the new leader's relationship with, and commitment from, this person, or potentially liberate the team member to find another role that is a better fit.

When one member of a peer group is elevated to a player-coach role, they must recognize that their relationship with the group members will change, like it or not. The leader is no longer a regular member of the team, but is now responsible for evaluating each individual and the performance of the team, assign work, etc. It helps for the player-coach to establish some expectations with the team in a humble but firm fashion to make the transition easier for everyone, and to recognize and encourage the team so they know they have the player-coach's support, and the support of others. Anything the player-coach says or does should not be about them, but about the team and its role in the overall organization.

It's common for team members in player roles to talk about other members of the team, which is something a player-coach should never do. This is a new relationship with the team, and the player-coach needs to take stock of it and how to manage it. Most importantly, the new leader should never lose their humility (it's not all about them and their new role) or courage (to make decisions that need to be made).

From external hire to player-coach. In this case, the team knows one another, but they don't know the player-coach, and the player-coach doesn't know them. The player-coach may have experience leading teams, but not leading *this* team.

Immediately after stepping into the role of player-coach, the new hire must get to know each member of the team. It is likely not possible to sum them up after one or two meetings, but the new player-coach should quickly become familiar with each player, reflecting on questions like:

- What are this person's skills, and are they a great fit for the role they are in or not?
- What is their interaction like with the rest of the team—are they a contributor or a detractor?
- Does this person have a full workload, or is there more they can do?
- What are their desires and aspirations?

By gathering this information, the player-coach will be able to identify if team members are in the right role and on the right team, then they can start planning for how to help them grow in their roles and/or beyond.

Often, new player-coaches want to immediately start building team spirit and trust among team members by doing things together, or through team-building exercises and events. A new player-coach can get ahead of themselves if they start to build team spirit and trust before properly analyzing the team and assessing if can accomplish the task, or if changes in skill sets and capabilities are needed. Starting to build the trust of a team whose composition is likely to change can be a waste of time, energy, and resources. We have always followed the adage "identify the team you need and build the trust among that team." You can imagine the potential negative impact on a team if you build a cohesive and trusting team first, and then change out some of the players.

A newly hired or transferred player-coach has work to do beyond getting to know their team. They also must identify the contacts and colleagues they need to form strong relationships with in order for the team to flourish: internal clients, partners (colleagues in adjacent functions or related functions), or staff who support or work closely with the team. In our transition coaching, we like to say "identify who can make you or break you" and build relationships with them. It is also about pinpointing who is instrumental in making the team successful.

While the player-coach is meeting people and forming relationships, they need to be cognizant of how the team and function are viewed. The new leader may be able to identify low-hanging fruit to act on in order to strengthen the impression others have of the team. Getting some quick wins for the team as a new leader can build credibility and capital—both of which will be valuable when it comes time to attack the major issues.

From solo player to player-coach of a group. In some ways, it is easier for a player who grows a team and becomes a player-coach in the process to establish their leadership role within the team. Of course, that ease is offset by the efforts required to recruit and select the members of the team.

If growing the team from scratch, so to speak, the player-coach must recognize the importance of each hire: each new member should bring something to the table that will add to the team. The player-coach should be looking for quality hires who have the potential to eventually step into the leadership role. It is troubling to think there are leaders who think differently than this, but we have encountered far too many player-coaches who want to hire team members who are not as good as they are to ensure their job is safe. While it may appear that without a strong successor the player-coach's job is safe, it is actually more at risk if the team doesn't perform well. The player-coach should surround themselves with the best talent they can find and with people who can work together.

We say the transition in this scenario is a little easier because new hires to the team will already look at the new player-coach as the authority figure—the leader won't have to prove themselves and earn the role in quite the same way as in the first two transition scenarios. Nonetheless, the player-coach will be onstage with every new member, so they still need to play the leadership role well.

Coaching player-coaches

An effective player-coach may be given a further promotion so that they have direct reports who also have direct reports: they are the *leader* of player-coaches. This introduces some new dynamics that the leader should be aware of. In this section, we will use the term 'leader' to refer to the coach of player-coaches. Virtually all of the advice we provide applies to any leader who has other people leaders reporting to them.

The way that the leader interacts with people who are not their direct reports can reinforce those employees' reporting relationship with their manager or weaken their reporting relationship. The leader should never do anything that will undermine the authority or the role of their direct reports. It is easy to do this unintentionally, especially if a direct report is a relatively new player-coach who may not be fulfilling all of the responsibilities of their role yet. The leader must always keep in mind that, for the player-coach to be effective, the leader can't just pick up the work for them: they must invest in their player-coaches. This doesn't mean that the leader can't interact *at all* with employees who are two levels down, but their main role is to recognize and build their direct reports—or why have them? The leader should keep their direct reports informed of any interactions with the direct reports' team members to ensure they are on the same page and the player-coach can reinforce what is said, and vice versa.

For the most part, the leader does not need to give day-to-day direction to a direct report's team—that is for the player-coach to do. This doesn't mean the leader can't go directly to someone else's direct report for an answer or an action: a leader should always be able to go directly to the person who most likely has the answer. But any leader should respect the structure of their organization. For example, if requesting information from someone two levels down, the leader could suggest that that person touch base with their direct leader to let them know about the request. The leader could also follow up with the player-coach to ensure they're both on the same page. This shows that the leader does not intend to leave their direct report out of the picture.

Sometimes a leader may find that a direct report, a player-coach, is not adequately leading. In this case, the leader must invest in coaching the player-coach to build their skills and awareness, and this must be done without disparaging them in any way.

If the leader receives complaints about one of their player-coach's leadership, they should listen to the complaint, and then advise the team member to share their feedback with their direct manager. The exception to this is any behavior from the player-coach that implies harassment; managing by fear, discrimination, unethical or illegal behavior; or any grave departure from the values or policies of the company. If the complaint falls into any of those areas, the leader should thank the team member for sharing the information, then tell them that they will need to investigate the situation and get back to them soon. The leader should not dismiss these complaints, nor should they side with the team member without further information. The leader must take any such complaint seriously and diligently follow up on it. They must inform the player-coach about the complaint against them and give them the opportunity to explain themselves. The leader should also try to corroborate the story with others who may have evidence. This is an area where reaching out to HR is a smart decision.

It is crucial for the leader to be an advocate, mentor, and an advisor on career development for both their direct reports *and* those reporting to them. We know several inspiring leaders who have regular (but not necessarily frequent) check-ins to understand every team member's aspirations, what they are working on regarding skills and career, and the support and assistance they might need.

Leaders are also the reminders and carriers of the organization's direction and values. They embody the culture of the organization and the rules of the road through their interactions and communications with the team. A conflict between communication and behavior will confuse and dilute any message the leader wants to send.

The majority of a leader's time should generally be spent on their direct reports. The more they can coach their team and keep them going in the right direction, the better the overall team will function. A seasoned player-coach-turned-executive gave us some great insight: "When things were not going right, everyone seemed to be working one layer down in the organization. If I noticed they were having to work two levels down, it was always a people issue that had to be resolved." This was an excellent perspective on how leaders compensate or take on others' work when things are not going well—and for some, it takes a while to get back to recover. "Rather than continuing to focus down in the organization, identify who is the issue and quickly make the decision as to whether it is a coachable situation or you are in need of a talent change," he added.

Just as someone making the transition from player to player-coach has to lift their perspective and role, a more senior player-coach who is leading other player-coaches must continue to broaden their perspective, consider a longer-term view, and perform in the leadership role for the organization to be the best it can be.

Supporting player-coaches

Those who are in roles supporting a player-coach—human resources professionals, mentors, or internal consultants—can help the player-coach focus on pure leadership. To do so effectively, it helps to use a particular model of leadership—whether it is our model or not—and reinforce the player-coach's actions that are consistent with that model.

For those supporting a player-coach:

- You may provide feedback that others may not be willing to give. You must be willing to share insight on the player-coach's actions and what you are hearing in terms of how they are coming across to their team.

- You can help them focus their time on the critical aspects of the role. Ronald Heifetz, from the Kennedy School at Harvard, reminds us that the leader's most valuable capital is their time.[24] You want to help the leader spend their time (capital) on whatever is most important to their team and organization.

- You can assist by holding them accountable on difficult issues that seem to drag on if no one else is willing to face the awkward and difficult moment—you can help them face those challenges. We have seen instances where the player-coach or leader will lean on HR or another business partner to do some of that awkward and messy work for them. If you support a player-coach or leader who asks that of you, you can help them—somewhat. It won't be as helpful or impactful as helping them *face it and learn to face it again*. That is not easy, but in terms of coaching and helping, this is the higher calling than doing the 'dirty work' for them.

- You can help them see themselves in a mirror by way of your feedback and observations; you can help them polish the rough edges or improve their actions.

- If you are supporting a player-coach from a role in HR, you can assist them with access to programs, processes, and resources to help them as leaders as well as to help their team grow. Often these resources are easy to access if you work with them routinely, but they can be a black hole to those who don't access them regularly. Helping the player coach access and know what is available can pay huge dividends for both parties.

Supporters can help player-coaches realize that their role is pivotal to how their leadership will be viewed in the future. If they can gain the confidence and capability to effectively lead, their impact will increase exponentially.

To those supporting multi-tiered organizations, it's important to help the top leader focus on their personal role and not the leaders below them. It is also important to recognize the role of the top leader by helping them hone their focus on their role and not the role of their direct reports or players. This does not mean you hide from them or guard information of what is happening in their organization, it means acting as a filter and helping them prioritize what they should get involved in and what they should be delegating. For example, reminding them that any employee issues two levels down from the leader should be handled by their direct reports. In some cases, the leader may have to get involved but help them play their role, not the role of those within their organization.

While experience is an essential component to a leader's development, relationships with others can also be incredible growth opportunities in terms of learning best practices, understanding different perspectives, gaining new ideas, or building on ideas. Three specific aspects of relationships are particularly helpful: mentorship/sponsorship, internal networks, and external networks. Let's explore each of these briefly.

Mentorship/sponsorship. Mentorship can help a player-coach benefit from the experiences of others who have been through the very challenges the player-coach is facing. The word 'mentor' actually comes from the story of Mentor in Homer's *Odyssey*. Odysseus, King of Ithaca, entrusts the care of his son, Telemachus, to Mentor when he goes to fight in the Trojan War. Mentor served as teacher and overseer of Odysseus' son, and the term 'mentor' has come to be defined as a trusted advisor, teacher, and wise person. A good mentor can help an individual see things from a different perspective, assist by telling of their own experience in similar situations, and help the mentee avoid some of the same mistakes or issues.

Often organizations have formal mentorship programs and senior leaders serve as mentors to junior leaders—in terms of tenure or level in the organization. These mentoring relationships usually last six months to a year, with monthly meetings. We know many leaders who are actively mentoring multiple employees at the same time, and we have seen great lessons learned and many people who have benefited from such programs. We believe player-coaches should be open and even proactive to the concept of mentorship.

In our corporate lives, we nurtured and supported mentoring programs and found an interesting phenomenon: many of the high-potential participants we were matching with a mentor were interested in, and lobbied for, being mentored by what we will term 'celebrity' mentors. They wanted to be mentored by the CEO, or one of the top leaders in the organization who was dynamic and often had substantial exposure in front of both employees and the public. Our experience with such programs helped us understand that sometimes the most outstanding mentors were not the sought-after celebrities, but the leaders who were a little more in the background yet had tons of wisdom, and a style that really encouraged and nurtured learning.

The lesson here is that mentoring is about more than exposure to a leader: this exposure is positive and can be meaningful, but it is not the only purpose of mentorship. All leaders should be expected to mentor and to stretch a hand down in the organization to help those rising and climbing to learn. They should be proactive in identifying talent and mentoring instead of waiting for it to be programmatically placed in their laps.

A word to all those who participate in a mentoring relationship—the responsibility for shaping the relationship flows both ways. It should not be the mentor simply dictating what the mentee should learn. In fact, we believe that in a mentoring relationship the mentee should be responsible for the bulk of the agenda and preparation. The mentor may outline what he or she feels are critical areas to explore, but the mentee should come prepared with questions and topics for discussion. It is not a 'sit at the feet and just listen' kind of relationship, but one where the mentee helps shape the conversation to gain the most out of it.

We usually think of a mentorship as a senior executive (mentor) and a junior executive (mentee), but we have also seen some very effective examples of 'reverse mentoring,' where the junior executive will teach and help answer questions from the senior executive in areas where the junior executive is much more experienced or has more knowledge. This concept has been used effectively in larger companies to help senior leaders learn of and understand better such things as technology and social media. We highly encourage creativity when designing mentoring relationships.

'Sponsorship' is another word often used synonymously with mentoring: but it doesn't mean the exact same thing. On occasion mentors (programmatically established or organically established) may become sponsors for a rising leader. When someone becomes a sponsor for someone else, they are not only sharing their experiences and knowledge, but actively involved in the other person's career and next steps. Sponsors advocate for someone's work product, their next assignments, their character, and their potential, even when the other person is not present. Sponsors are willing to open up their personal network. Sponsorship tends to happen over time and is not scheduled or event-based.

Internal networks. We encourage all player-coaches to establish an internal network of individuals whom they regularly meet with and learn from. This network should extend beyond the player-coach's function and include different levels and types of people. This internal network will do several things for the individual. First, it will expand their perspective beyond the narrow niche that they may serve, helping them learn about other functions and more about the company as a whole. Second, it will help give them insight into how things actually get accomplished within the company, and why it may take longer or require more steps than one might originally think necessary. Finally, it is an avenue for the player-coach to get things done across functions faster, and with higher quality, because of the relationships that are formed.

We need more than our combined twenty fingers to count the number of clients we have worked with who have said, "Things get done through relationships here." Most of the clients who have mentioned this think their company is unique, but we find in most companies the ability to get something done across functions is heavily dependent on the relationships and network of the individual trying to get something done. Internal networks are valuable for development *and* in performance.

We have seen many managers and leaders who are very good at this, and the common thread among them is that it is intentional. They regularly reach out for lunch, a drink after work, or a breakfast before work with countless people across many functions. Sometimes these relationships go beyond work. Not all internal relationships have to become that tight, but the most effective networkers connect on a fairly regular basis and they do not neglect the health of their network. These strong networkers know that it is a two-way street: if their partners in the network sense one-sidedness, the relationship will prove fruitless.

WISDOM FROM OUTSIDE THE COCOON

WHEN I WAS selected to spearhead the leadership education function in my company, the departing leader said, "90 percent of your success will depend on the strength of your external network." At the time, I took his word on faith because I didn't really see the value. After a few years on the job I fully understood what he was saying as the role called for bringing new ideas and up-to-date perspectives to our leaders in the organization. Fortunately for me, my predecessor had established a network and pattern for the role and I was instantly introduced to a network of peers across the globe.

TAMMY

External networks. Just as internal networks are critical, strong external networks are essential for broadening perspective and furthering professional development. External networks can inspire new perspectives on the business that may not arise if the player-coach is only internally focused. In an external network that is functionally focused, the player-coach will learn new and different perspectives on their function. Even better is a network that expands a bit beyond a particular function, so the player-coach can stretch and grow from the exposure. External networks can strengthen a player-coach's confidence to engage with and support peers beyond their company who are facing similar challenges.

As with the internal network, an external network has to be a two-way street, one in which the player-coach is giving—answering questions, providing support to others—as well as receiving. And as a player-coach leads others, they should encourage their team members to develop their own internal and external networks to grow professionally.

"All coaching is, is taking a player where he can't take himself."

BILL MCCARTNEY, FORMER AMERICAN
FOOTBALL PLAYER AND COACH[25]

Set Direction

- Understand expectations
- Make plans
- Prioritize
- Set objectives and expectations
- Communicate for alignment
- Reflect and adjust
- Create a vision for the future

Secure Resources

- Identify resource requirements
- Assess existing resources
- Identify interdependencies
- Acquire funding and other resources
- Put talent in the best places
- Constantly remove roadblocks

Build Team

- Communicate to inspire
- Leverage the team
- Motivate
- Recognize
- Build trust

Coach Individuals

- Observe and learn
- Listen and understand
- Coach and develop
- Give ongoing feedback
- Hold individuals accountable
- Stretch and motivate

CLOSING

WHETHER YOU ARE preparing for a player-coach role, are a newly promoted or a more experienced player-coach who is now leading others, or someone in a support role to a player-coach, we hope this book was helpful to your task at hand. We realize this is not a comprehensive, research-based book on leadership, but our goal has been to provide basic, practical thoughts on the concept of the player-coach based on the experience we have garnered through dynamic, rewarding, and rich in careers in business. If this book benefits your career trajectory, smoothens your transition between roles, or improves your leadership tactics, we are delighted.

If you are a player-coach who is motivated to put some of our lessons into practice, here are some final tips on how to get started.

First, identify one or two areas to focus on. You may want to improve in five or six areas, but if you spread your focus across many areas, you will dilute your efforts and make little progress. Pick *one or two* areas to focus on for a few months. As you begin to feel more comfortable and effective in those areas, and new actions and practices become internalized and part of your habits, pick up another area to focus on. *Don't try to attack every area at once.*

Second, don't grow alone, 'hang the marquee.' Old movie theaters used to have big marquees hanging outside, complete with flashing lights, to announce the movie that was currently showing. We encourage you to let others in on your development desires and check in with them from time. Ask them for 'feedforward' or suggestions on what you might do to improve in a specific area. This technique creates accountability: you've told people you want to make certain changes, and you are checking in to see if change is happening. You may also pick up some great ideas or suggestions about growing your skills and behaviors from those who may actually be impacted by them.

Third, make a very specific plan of actions you will take, and the behaviors you will demonstrate. We often hear of folks who want to 'get better' at something, but until they map out the action, they are just hoping they will get better. In your plan, make sure you build in actions on almost a daily basis if you are serious about growing and changing your behavior. The more frequently you can practice a behavior, the more likely it will be to become habit and comfortable.

At the beginning of this chapter is our complete player-coach success model to help you identify your primary areas of focus and to incubate a plan.

You can use this model to identify where you want to put your effort. Reflect on questions like, "Where am I already strong? Where do I want to get better?" Where you are strong, you want to ensure that you reinforce and leverage those strengths. Where you want to grow, put your efforts into really improving in those areas.

Start being more mindful of your time. In any given week, identify how much time you spend on the following activities:

- monitoring or motivating those you lead;
- coaching and teaching those you lead;
- planning for your team and their development;
- focusing on your development as a leader;
- ensuring resources and removing roadblocks for those you lead; and
- planning for your function.

Assess where you are spending your time on a daily basis, and consider what your specific role requires of you at any given moment, so you are able to make effective shifts in your time management. Where you are spending your time today based on organizational needs may need to change every month, every quarter, or annually, so establish a routine time-frame to reassess on a regular basis.

Finally, we encourage you to continue your journey of growth as a leader. Your opportunity to bless the lives of others and assist in their journeys is what leadership is all about. We all benefit from those who have gone before us. You can say we 'sit in the shade of trees we did not plant.' As a leader, your contribution is to plant and nurture trees to provide shade and benefit for others. It is our hope that we have been able to contribute in some way to that shade.

"Management is the most noble of professions if it's practiced well. No other occupation offers as many ways to help others learn and grow, take responsibility and be recognized for achievement, and contribute to the success of a team. More and more MBA students come to school thinking that a career in business means buying, selling, and investing in companies. That's unfortunate. Doing deals doesn't yield the deep rewards that come from building up people."

CLAYTON CHRISTENSEN,
HARVARD BUSINESS SCHOOL PROFESSOR[26]

NOTES

1 Many of the facts about Bill Russell's career in this section are drawn from "Bill Russell," Wikipedia, https://en.wikipedia.org/wiki/Bill_Russell, accessed April 2019.

2 Malcolm Gladwell, *Outliers: The Story of Success* (Little, Brown and Company, 2008). A common theme that appears throughout *Outliers* is the '10,000-Hour Rule,' based on a study by Anders Ericsson.

3 Liz Wiseman with Greg McKeown, *Multipliers: How the Best Leaders Make Everyone Smarter* (HarperCollins, 2010). In this book, Wiseman and McKeown look at various types of leaders and identify two different types: Multipliers and Diminishers. Multipliers are leaders who encourage growth and creativity from their workers, while Diminishers are those who hinder and otherwise keep their employees' productivity at a minimum. The authors give what they consider to be solutions and guidance to the issues they bring up in the book.

4 Jim Clifton quoted in Victor Lipman, *The Type B Manager: Leading Successfully in a Type A World* (Penguin Group, 2015).

5 Denis Waitley, https://www.goodreads.com/author/quotes/5108.Denis_Waitley?page=2, accessed April 2019. Denis is an American author and public speaker.

6 Rodd Wagner and Jim Harter, "The Second Element of Great Managing," Gallup, https://news.gallup.com/businessjournal/27115/The-Second-Element _of-Great-Managing.aspx, accessed April 2019.

7   Patrick Lencioni, *The Five Dysfunctions of a Team: A Leadership Fable* (Jossey-Bass, 2002). References also found at https://www.tablegroup .com/books/dysfunctions. See Dysfunction #5.

8   Jim C. Collins, *Good to Great: Why Some Companies Make the Leap . . . and Others Don't* (HarperBusiness, 2001).

9   Collins, *Good to Great.*

10   Jessica Glazer, "The Forgotten Influence of Your Personal Life and Hardships on Leadership," www.ccl.org, accessed April 2019. There is some evidence that the model was actually developed prior to and independently from the CCL research. Professor Allen Tough, a psychologist and expert on adult learning and self-directed growth, referred to a similar perspective in his work a decade earlier. While the origin of the model is in question, it has been overwhelmingly adopted and/or adapted by talent management and learning professionals globally. There is some question as to its technical accuracy or supporting research, but little question about its acceptance, popularity, and use.

11   Morgan McCall Jr., Michael Lombardo, and Ann Morrison, *The Lessons of Experience: How Successful Executives Develop on the Job* (Lexington Books, 1988).

12   Kim Scott, *Radical Candor: Be a Kick-Ass Boss without Losing Your Humanity* (St. Martin Press, 2017). Radical Candor™ is the ability to challenge directly and show you care personally at the same time. *Radical Candor* will help you and all the people you work with do the best work of your lives and build the best relationships of your career.

13   Jeff Thompson, MD, *Lead True: Live Your Values, Build Your People, Inspire Your Community* (ForbesBooks, 2017).

14   Claire Tristram, "Wanna Be a Player? Get a Coach!" *Fast Company,* https://www.fastcompany.com/27767/wanna-be-player-get-coach, accessed April 2019.

15   Babe Ruth, https://www.brainyquote.com/quotes/babe_ruth_125974, accessed April 2019.

16   Marshall Goldsmith, "Try Feedforward Instead of Feedback," https://
     www.marshallgoldsmith.com/articles/try-feedforward-instead-feed
     back/, accessed April 2019.

17   Edward M. Hallowell, *CrazyBusy: Overstretched, Overbooked,
     and About to Snap! Strategies for Handling Your Fast-Paced Life*
     (Ballantine Books, 2007).

18   Boyd Clark and Ron Crossland, *The Leader's Voice: How Your
     Communication Can Inspire Action and Get Results* (Tom Peters
     and Select Books, Inc., 2002).

19   Justin Bariso, "This Email from Elon Musk to Tesla Employees Describes
     What Great Communication Looks Like," *Inc.*, https://www.inc.com/
     justin-bariso/this-email-from-elon-musk-to-tesla-employees-descr.html,
     accessed April 2019.

20   Francis J. Flynn and J. Brockner. (2003). "It's Different to Give Than
     to Receive: Asymmetric Reactions of Givers and Receivers to Favor
     Exchange." *Journal of Applied Psychology*, 88(6): 1–13.

21   Quoted in "The Ben Franklin Effect," Farnam Street Media, https://
     fs.blog/2011/07/the-ben-franklin-effect/.

22   David Allen, *Getting Things Done: The Art of Stress-Free Productivity*
     (Viking, 2001). Michael D. Watkins, *The First 90 Days: Proven
     Strategies for Getting Up to Speed Faster and Smarter* (Harvard Business
     Review, 2013).

23   Yehuda Berg, "The Power of Words," *HuffPost*, https://www.huffpost.
     com/entry/the-power-of-words_n_716183, accessed April 2019.

24   Ronald A. Heifetz and Donald L. Laurie. (2001, December). "The Work
     of Leadership," *Harvard Business Review*, https://hbr.org/2001/12/
     the-work-of-leadership, accessed July 2019.

25   Bill McCartney, https://www.brainyquote.com/quotes/bill_mccart
     ney_381122, accessed April 2019.

26   Clayton M. Christensen. (2010, July–August). "How Will You Measure
     Your Life?" *Harvard Business Review*, https://hbr.org/2010/07/
     how-will-you-measure-your-life, accessed July 2019.

ABOUT THE AUTHORS

VAL MARKOS AND TAMMY MARTIN worked together for over ten years in human resources at BellSouth Corporation, now AT&T Inc. Their philosophies paralleled nicely, and they frequently collaborated over the years in a variety of different roles, focusing on talent management, succession planning, and organizational development. When Val left BellSouth in 2006, Tammy continued working in leadership development and human resources leadership during and after the merger with AT&T.

Tammy was born and raised in Georgia and has traveled frequently all over the United States for work. She received her bachelor of arts in journalism from the University of Georgia and began her professional career as a graphic artist. She was hired by BellSouth Corporation in 1986 and served in various leadership roles with increasing responsibility over her thirty-year career with BellSouth and AT&T. She spent the bulk of her tenure in human resource management and leadership development, where her passion was working with leaders across the company to excel at leading others. Tammy established The 5 Eleven Group in early 2018, a company focused on leadership consulting and executive coaching. When she isn't working, Tammy enjoys the outdoors, music, cooking, painting, and giving of her time to others, especially her son, Drew, and her church. Tammy and her husband, Andy, now live part time in Georgia and part time in Western North Carolina where they enjoy the outdoors and relaxed culture.

Val is originally from Utah and spent most of his youth there, finally leaving the Wasatch Range to attend graduate school at the University of Georgia (UGA). After spending four years (to the day!) at UGA, he left with a PhD and went to work applying his education to roles at City of Miami, Florida; U.S. Steel; and then at BellSouth where he was executive director of leadership development. Since 2006 Val has worked as principal at Vmark Consulting doing just what he loves to do: coaching executives and providing assessment services for the development and selection of leadership roles. Val and his wife, Blanche, are empty-nesters with three children and ten grandchildren spread from coast to coast. Val is an avid cyclist and sports fan. He is heavily committed to his community and his faith.

FOR MORE ON

PLAYER-COACH LEADERSHIP

VISIT US AT
www.playercoachleadership.com

OR EMAIL US DIRECTLY AT
info@playercoachleadership.com